SEE & EXPLORE
LIBRARY

FLIGHT
and FLYING MACHINES

Written by
Steve Parker

Illustrated by
Luciano Corbella

DORLING KINDERSLEY, INC.
LONDON · NEW YORK · STUTTGART

A DORLING KINDERSLEY BOOK

Editor Miranda Smith
Art editor Chris Scollen
Designer Richard Cane

Managing art editor Roger Priddy
Series editor Angela Wilkes
Editorial director Sue Unstead
Production controller Louise Barratt

Contributing illustrators
Dave Pugh, Studio B,
Kevin Maddison, Kevin Lyles, Peter Ross,
Robert Garrard, Hussein Hussein

Revised American Edition, 1993
10 9 8 7 6 5 4 3 2 1

Published in the United States by
Dorling Kindersley, Inc., 232 Madison Avenue
New York, New York 10016

Copyright © 1990
Dorling Kindersley Limited, London

ISBN 1-56458-236-1

Library of Congress Catalog Card
Number 92-54316

Phototypset by SX Composing Ltd, Rayleigh, England
Color separations by DOT Gradations Limited
Printed in Spain by Artes Graficas, Toledo S.A.

D L TO: 1786-1992

CONTENTS

HIGH IN THE SKY

To ground-bound creatures such as ourselves, the sky seems very big and empty. Indeed, it *is* big – but not empty. Around the Earth is a blanket of air called the "atmosphere." This air weighs over 5,000 million million tons and is made up of a mixture of gases, mainly nitrogen and oxygen. We cannot see, smell, or taste air. But we can feel it when the wind blows on our faces, because wind is moving air.

If air was not there, we could not fly. Flight is made possible by pushing against air. The air "pushes back" with enough force to lift the flyer off the ground. True flight means moving through the air, without touching the land, in a controlled way, and for a reasonable time. A leaf blowing in the wind is not really flying, since it has no control over where it goes, and it soon falls to the ground. Insects, birds, and bats are the only animals capable of true flight, on their own. Humans can fly, too, but we need the help of machines. Our inventiveness and ingenuity have filled the skies with all manner of flying machines that float, soar, glide, and roar.

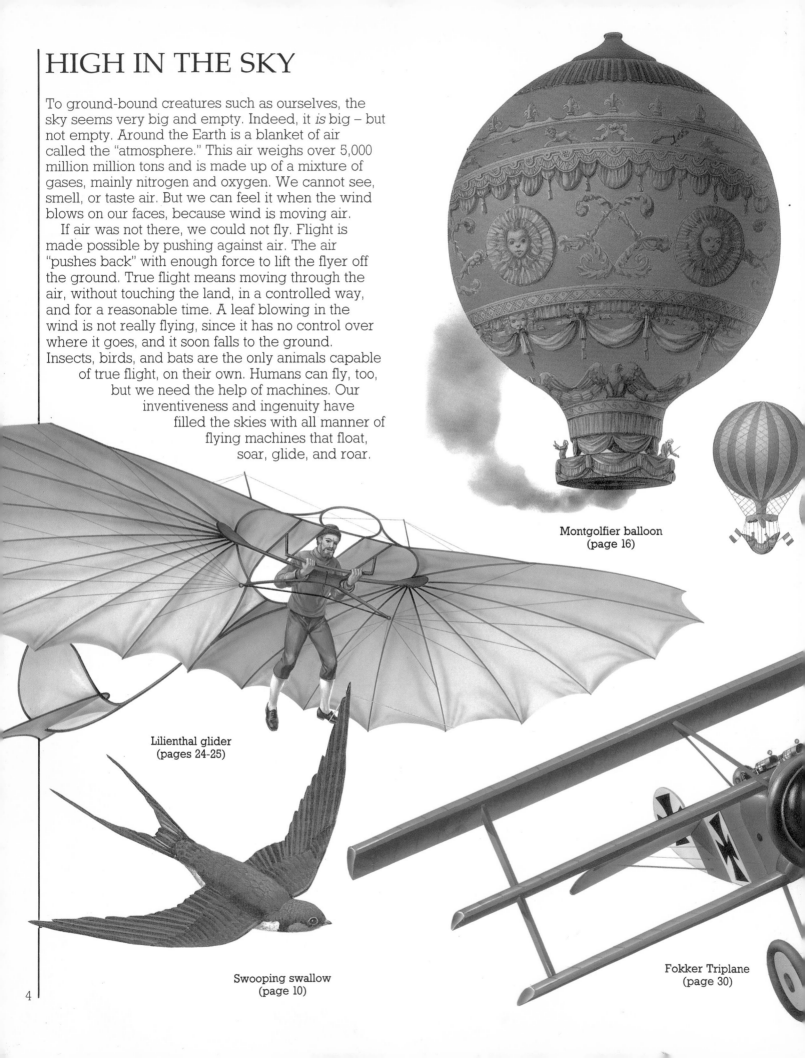

Montgolfier balloon
(page 16)

Lilienthal glider
(pages 24-25)

Swooping swallow
(page 10)

Fokker Triplane
(page 30)

4

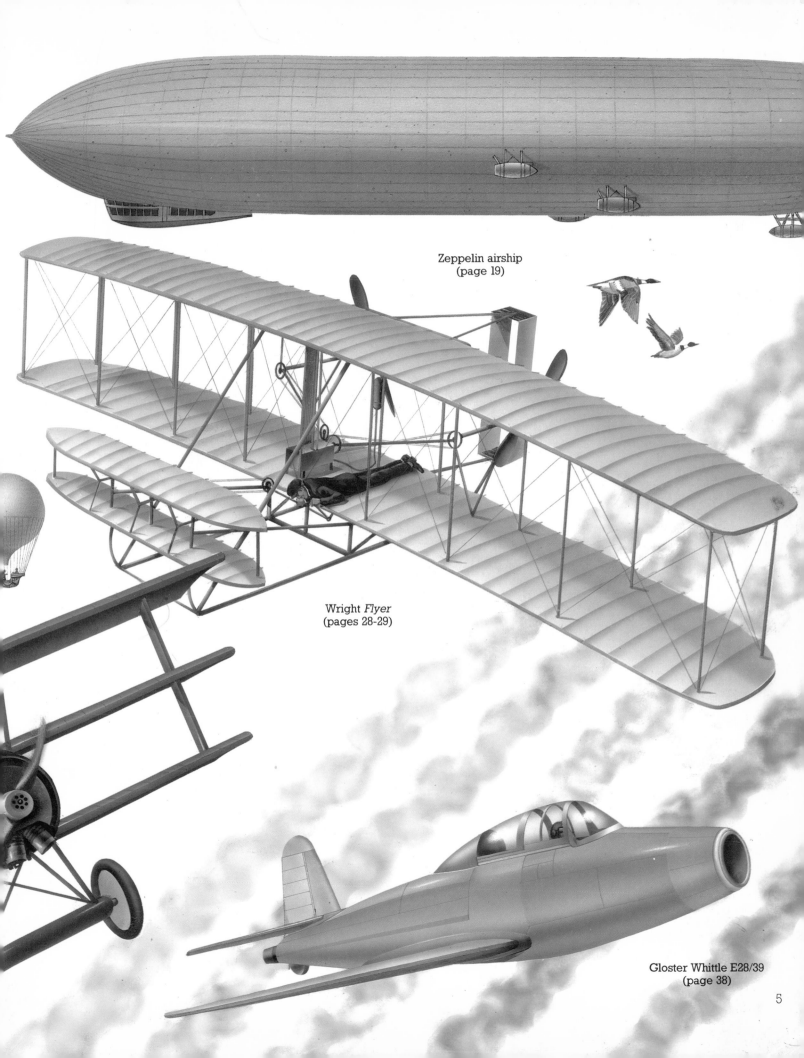

Zeppelin airship
(page 19)

Wright *Flyer*
(pages 28-29)

Gloster Whittle E28/39
(page 38)

Speeds in the sky

One of the most important features of a flying machine is how fast it goes. Helicopters are useful because they can simply hover in mid-air. Concorde's advantage is its great speed. It is "supersonic," which means it can go through the "sound barrier" and fly faster than the speed of sound (about 760 mph, or 1,225 kph, at sea level).

Jet aerobatic team
(pages 46-47)

Colorful kite
(page 20)

Steerable parachute
(pages 22-23)

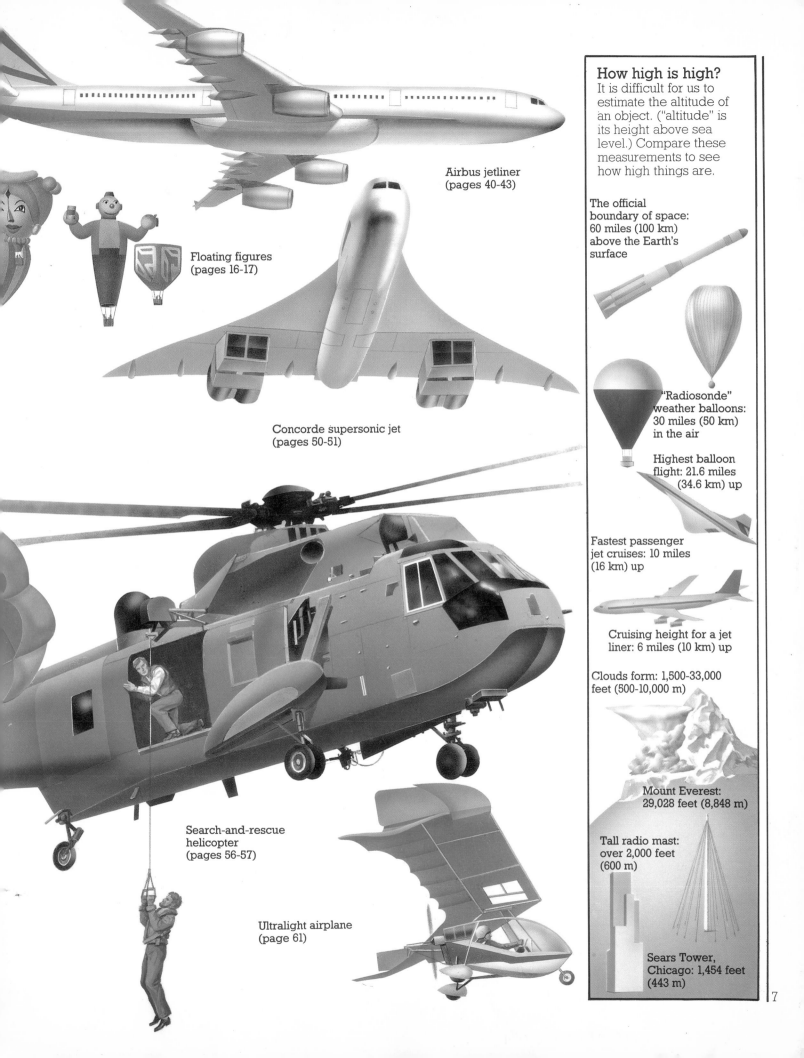

Airbus jetliner
(pages 40-43)

Floating figures
(pages 16-17)

Concorde supersonic jet
(pages 50-51)

Search-and-rescue
helicopter
(pages 56-57)

Ultralight airplane
(page 61)

How high is high?

It is difficult for us to estimate the altitude of an object. ("altitude" is its height above sea level.) Compare these measurements to see how high things are.

The official boundary of space: 60 miles (100 km) above the Earth's surface

"Radiosonde" weather balloons: 30 miles (50 km) in the air

Highest balloon flight: 21.6 miles (34.6 km) up

Fastest passenger jet cruises: 10 miles (16 km) up

Cruising height for a jet liner: 6 miles (10 km) up

Clouds form: 1,500-33,000 feet (500-10,000 m)

Mount Everest: 29,028 feet (8,848 m)

Tall radio mast: over 2,000 feet (600 m)

Sears Tower, Chicago: 1,454 feet (443 m)

FLYING LIKE A BIRD

The first animals evolved in the sea, in the distant prehistoric past. Then, about 350-400 million years ago, the first land creatures crawled on to the shore. Next, the first flying creatures took to the air.

Through the ages, four main groups of animals have mastered flight. Leading the way were insects, which buzzed through the great coal swamps over 300 million years ago. Next, about 200 million years ago, came the pterosaurs, or flying reptiles. However, these died out with the dinosaurs, 65 million years ago. About 150 million years ago, birds began to flap through the air. Finally, over 50 million years ago, bats appeared on the scene. All these creatures have been shaped by evolution for flying. They have broad, flat wings, which are flapped by very powerful muscles. They have light bodies with many weight-saving features, such as hollow bones. The birds, bats, and insects can control their movements and go up, or down, or turn to one side. They differ from the gliding animals (page 27), which have less control and can only swoop downward.

Hunter on the wing

The fish eagle, or osprey, is a master of flight. Like most birds it can rise, dive, turn, and soar at will. Its front limbs have evolved into wings, flapped by powerful muscles in the chest. On their down stroke, the wings force the air backward and downward, which pushes the bird forward and upward.

Primary flight feathers

Flight feathers
The main wing feathers are the primaries, which are near the wing's tip, and the secondaries, near the body. The large vanes of the feathers overlap to give a wide, flat, airtight surface that pushes air efficiently.

Secondary flight feathers

Tail feathers
The bird can spread and twist its feathers in order to control its flying speed and direction. The tail is spread to form an "air brake" whenever the bird slows down, hovers, or lands.

Airborne insects
Flying insects include butterflies, moths, gnats, beetles, and the "fly" itself. Their wings are made of flat sheets of a skinlike material, called wing membranes. These are stiffened by tubes known as veins. The wings connect to the central part of the body, the thorax. A small insect like a mosquito flaps its wings at over 500 beats each second!

Up stroke

Colorful wings
Butterfly and moth wings are covered in a mosaic of tiny colored scales. The beautiful patterns camouflage the insect, or help it recognize a mate.

Fly in flight
As a fly flaps its wings up and down, the wings also twist along their length. This gives lifting power on the down and up stroke.

The thorax contains the flight muscles.

Down stroke

Wing bones
A bird's bones are mostly hollow tubes, strong yet light. The inner wing bone, or humerus, is equivalent to our own upper arm bone. It is attached to the wing-beating muscles in the chest and back.

Wing joints
The bird's "elbows" allow the outer part of the wing to bend in relation to the inner part, curving the whole wing up or down for extra control. The main up-down wing movements are carried out at the shoulder joint.

Hand bones
The bird's "hand" has only three fingers, and these are very small and buried among the feathers. The wrist bones are also small and mostly joined solidly together.

Alula
The group of small feathers at the front outer tip of the wing is called the alula. The bird spreads these feathers in slow flight, to prevent it stalling and suddenly falling downward. The alula works in the same way as an aircraft's wing flaps (page 32).

Chest muscles
Most of the power for flapping comes from the pectoral muscles in the chest. They pull the wings down, which keeps the bird up in the air. Smaller muscles in the bird's back pull the wings up again.

Covert feathers
The coverts, on the wing's underside, shape the front edge of the wing into the main flight feathers. This gives a surface over which air can flow easily.

On the wing

There are about 9,000 kinds of birds in the world, and they come in many shapes and sizes. There are huge game birds that weigh nearly 44 pounds (20 kg) and can only just lumber into the air. Tiny hummingbirds weigh 10,000 times less, and dart about on wings which beat so fast that they are just a blur. The size and shape of a bird's wings show much about its flying abilities and way of life. Short stubby wings, which are wide from front to back, are designed for fast bursts of speed, and quick twists and turns. Long straight wings, which are narrow from front to back, are better for long periods of soaring and gliding.

Earthbound

Penguins, ostriches, kiwis, and ground parrots have lost their powers of flight and live an earthbound life. Indeed, the penguin's wings have become short, strong flippers that push against water, not air. Game birds, like grouse and pheasants, also spend much time on the ground.

The adult eagle's wingspan (the measurement from one outstretched wing tip to the other) is 2 yards (2 m).

Swallow

Scythe-shaped wings show that this bird is built for long periods of fast flying. The swallow even feeds on the wing, snapping up small flying insects as it swoops down.

Eagle

This hunter has wide, powerful wings and a large tail, both signs of a strong and aerobatic flyer. It can swoop down and carry away prey as large as a hare or fox, held in its very powerful talons.

Night flying

Most bats have good eyesight, but even they cannot see on a very dark night. So the bat uses a kind of "radar," called echolocation. It makes a series of high squeaks that spread out into the night air. The sounds bounce off objects, and the bat's keen ears pick up the returning echoes. From the echoes, the bat can work out the size and distance of the object.

These flying mammals only leave their roosts when it is dark.

Magpie

A woodland bird, the magpie has "all-purpose" wings that are not too long or narrow. It also displays an easily recognized long tail. The central feather of the tail is nearly 9½ inches (25 cm) long. The magpie flies in a series of swoops, flapping upward once and then gliding down several times.

Male pheasant

Sand grouse

Grouse spend most of the time on the ground. They are heavily built, with strong legs and large feet. They usually take to the air only in an emergency, flapping their short wings so fast that they make a whirring sound.

FLIGHTS OF FANCY

Through the ages, people have looked up into the sky and longed to fly like the birds. How marvelous it would be to take off into the air, to flee from your enemies, to cross the sea to strange new lands! There are many legends about early human fliers and "birdmen," but modern science tells us that these cannot be true.

Over the centuries, inventors have designed all sorts of ingenious flying machines, but all were destined to fail. This was partly because the inventors did not understand the scientific principles behind flight, and partly because they did not use the right source of power. Any attempt to copy the birds, by attaching flapping wings to a person's arms, was doomed. This is because, compared to body weight, human chest and arm muscles are far less powerful

Daedalus and Icarus

Greek myth tells how the inventor Daedalus was forced to design an underground maze called the Labyrinth to house the Minotaur, a creature half-man, half-bull. To escape, Daedalus and his son Icarus fashioned wings of birds' feathers stuck with wax. Icarus flew too high and the sun's heat melted the wax. He plunged to his death in the sea.

Eilmer of Malmesbury

Many religions have stories of flying beings and spirits. About the year 1000, a monk named Eilmer attempted to fly like an angel from the tower of Malmesbury Abbey, in England. The story goes that he managed to glide a short way on wings strapped to his arms, but on landing broke both his legs. He did not try again!

Leonardo's flying machine

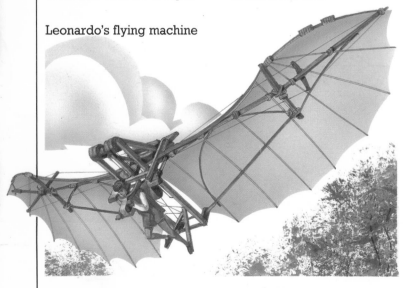

One of the greatest inventors of all time was the Italian, Leonardo da Vinci (1452-1519). He designed all kinds of machines. His flying machine, or "ornithopter," relied on flapping wings to stay in the air. This type of human-powered flight was later shown to be impossible by the biologist and engineer Giovanni Borelli, in 1685.

The Bishop's book

In 1638, Bishop Francis Godwin published *The Man in the Moon*. In the story, a nobleman tries to escape from an island by roping wild swans to a carriage. Unfortunately the swans were on their long migration flight. In those days people thought that they could travel all the way to the Moon, and that is exactly where the nobleman landed!

than a bird's. Human-powered flight has been achieved only in the past few years – and by using leg muscles, not arms.

Inventors who devised craft powered by engines also failed. This was usually because the engine was too heavy even to lift itself, let alone the pilot, craft, and fuel. The history of true powered flight began at the beginning of the 20th century (page 28).

(page 28)

Failures through the ages

This is a small selection of the many weird and wonderful "flying machine" designs of the past. Each craft is decorated in the style of its time. Some are human-driven, while others harness the power of the birds themselves. Sadly, none ever left the ground.

Gusmão's magnetic bird

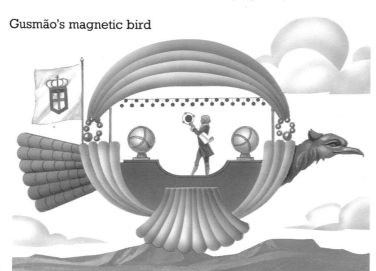

In 1709, Barthelemy Laurenco de Gusmão designed a craft to be lifted by magnets. At the time, magnetism was still a mysterious and little-understood force. Gusmão did not realize that iron was far too heavy, and its magnetic power too weak, for the machine to take off. He also added unnecessary weight in the form of flags and decorations.

Bréant's butterfly man

This 1854 creation used rubber bands to help with the flapping motion. The wings were in the shape of a butterfly – even down to the decorative eye-spots! It is true that a rubber band can hold energy, but this energy must first be "put into" the band by stretching it. The butterfly pilot's arm and shoulder muscles would have been much too weak.

Moy's rotator

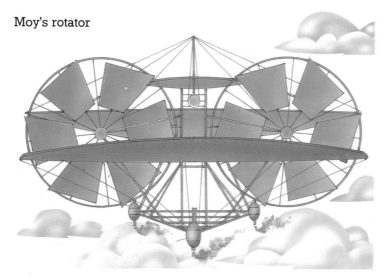

Thomas Moy made some of the first designs for flying machines based on scientific principles, in the 1860s. He chose a broad, flat, fixed wing, similar to that of a modern aircraft. His craft also had large rotating "propellers" to "propel" or push the machine forward. Like many others, he was unable to find a strong but light source of power.

Pedal power

This invention by Dr. W. Ayres, in 1885, had no wings at all. The power to lift the craft came from six small propellers, while a seventh drove it forwards. The pedals powered two lifting propellers, while the other four were turned by motors working on compressed air. The pilot had to turn the propeller using a handle, as well as work all the controls!

13

LIGHTER THAN AIR

The history of human flight began over 200 years ago. The first flying machine was a hot-air balloon, invented by the brothers Joseph and Jacques Montgolfier in France. It was made of sheets of cloth and paper, held together by stitches and buttons. A few weeks later, the brothers built a larger balloon and hung a basket below it on ropes. In the basket were a duck, a rooster, and a sheep, who took off and became the world's first air passengers! A few weeks after that, on October 15, 1783, an even larger Montgolfier balloon rose into the air with the first human flier, Jean-François Pilâtre de Rozier. To the cheers of the crowd, he flew to a height of 84 feet (25 m) and stayed aloft for almost four minutes. Within a few weeks, he made another trip, right over Paris (page 16). Today's balloons work in the same way as the early versions. Some use hot air created by a burner, like the one shown here. Others use special gases like helium, which are lighter than air.

A modern hot-air balloon

The balloon is the simplest flying machine. The pilot can control its height, making it go up or down, but that is all. The balloon will float wherever the wind blows it. However, a skillful balloonist knows that the wind direction varies with height, and with landscape features like hills and valleys. By altering height, he or she can sometimes "steer" in a certain direction. The wind direction also often changes at the coast or near a built-up area.

The envelope
The balloon's casing, or envelope, is made of tough, tear-proof material, such as nylon. It must be airtight, too, to stop the hot air leaking out. There is a heat-proof ring around the mouth, where the hot air rushes in. The envelope is made in sections for easy repair if the balloon snags on a tree or pylon.

Two-way radio for contact with ground crew

Anchor and rope

The basket
Some balloons carry their pilots in special capsules made of lightweight metal such as aluminum. But wicker baskets are still widely used for most sports and pleasure balloons. They are very light and strong, easy and cheap to make – and absorb the bump of a heavy landing!

The rise of hot air
The balloon idea came to the Montgolfier brothers when they watched smoke rise over a fire. The molecules, or particles, of air are further apart in hot air than in cool air. So hot air weighs less than the same volume of cool air. The brothers tried "trapping" hot air from a fire in a silk bag. Even with the weight of the silk, it was light enough to float upward. Gradually they devised a ball-shaped bag to hold the moist hot air.

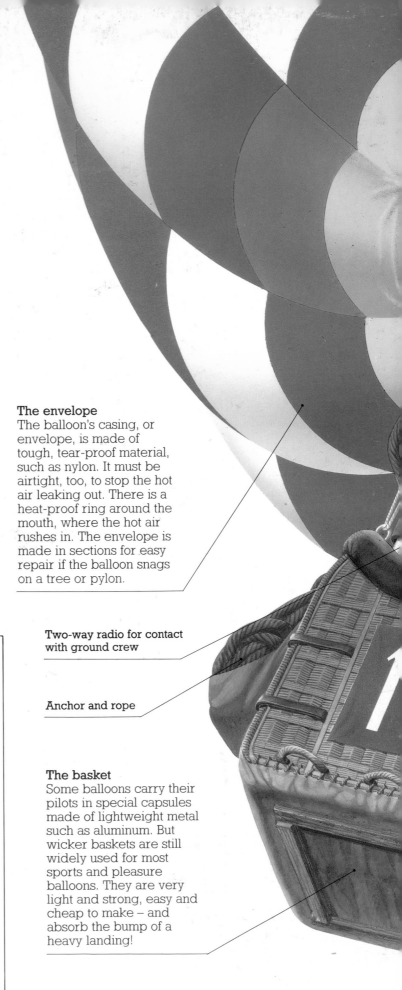

Valve
At the top of the envelope is a small hole, the valve. The pilot opens and closes this by pulling on a line. Opening the valve lets some hot air out of the envelope and so the balloon drifts down.

Ballast
On a normal take-off, the balloon carries extra weight or "ballast," such as sandbags. The pilot makes the balloon rise slowly by turning up the burner and making more hot air. But if he or she needs to go up quickly in an emergency (like avoiding a tall tree), the ballast is cut free. Suddenly the balloon is lighter and it rises rapidly.

The burner
Early hot-air balloons had fires stoked with wood or coal. The modern balloon has a powerful burner powered by gas in compressed gas bottles. The narrow flame sends hot air straight through the mouth into the envelope, with hardly any wastage.

Handles to steady basket and balloon during launch

BALLOONS AND AIRSHIPS

Two centuries ago, the first Montgolfier balloon rose into the air. Since then, balloons have been built in almost every shape and size, and for many purposes. Some carry no passengers but do important scientific work. In sport ballooning, contestants try to fly the farthest or stay aloft the longest.

Record breakers

Balloonists continually try to set distance and endurance records, and cross seas and mountains. The first balloon flight over the Atlantic Ocean was in 1978 by Double Eagle II. *The first balloon to cross the Pacific was* Double Eagle V *in 1981.*

Over the sea

Only two years after the Montgolfier flight, Jean Pierre Blanchard and Dr. John Jefferies flew across the Channel by balloon. They threw most of their clothes overboard to save weight, and they landed 12 miles (20 km) inland in their underwear!

The Age of Balloons begins

On November 21, 1783, Pilâtre de Rozier and the Marquis d'Arlandes floated across Paris in a gaily painted Montgolfier balloon. De Rozier had made "captive" flights (page 14), with the balloon tied to the ground by a long rope, but this was the first free flight.

Circus in the sky

Balloon flights soon became favorite events at fairs and festivals. In 1798, Monsieur Margat sat astride his splendid white stag, Coco, and floated over Paris, in a spectacular end to the annual festivities. France was the center of ballooning at this time.

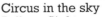

Silent flight
Balloons are very quiet compared to helicopters or airplanes. This makes them suitable for relaxing pleasure flights, especially "on safari." The balloon does not disturb the animals too much. It does not vibrate, either, making it easier to watch through binoculars or take good photographs.

Balloons in warfare
Soon after their invention, balloons were put to military use. In 1794 the French army used a balloon in the Battle of Fleurus against Austria. It was tied by a long rope, and observers surveyed the enemy positions to help the aim of the artillery.

Advertising balloons made in the shapes of their products.

Hi-tech balloons
Modern record-breaking balloons use the latest technology. In a pressurized aluminum capsule, pilots can reach great heights and use the fast-moving winds of the jet stream.

17

Ships of the air

It may not seem like a huge step from a free-floating balloon to a powered airship that can be controlled and steered. Yet the first airship did not fly until almost 70 years after the earliest balloons. These two types of flying machine differ in several ways.

Airships are powered by engines, and have a long, thin shape for stability. They are steered by movable panels, known as control surfaces. However, like balloons, they stay up because they contain lighter-than-air gas. In the 1930s, giant airships carried the first air passengers around the world in great luxury. But many airships contained the gas hydrogen, which burns easily, so they were at risk of fire. The passenger airship Hindenburg exploded in a ball of fire, killing 36 people. Modern airships use the gas helium. Like hydrogen, it is lighter than air, but it does not burn.

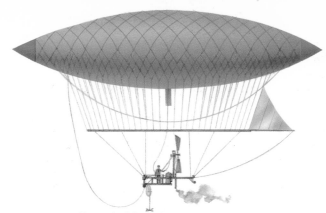

The first airship

A steam engine powered the first airship flight by Henri Giffard, a Frenchman, on September 24, 1852. The cigar-shaped balloon was filled with coal gas and contained in a net, with the engine, fuel, and pilot slung below. The balloon's volume was 88,287 cubic feet (2,500 cu m).

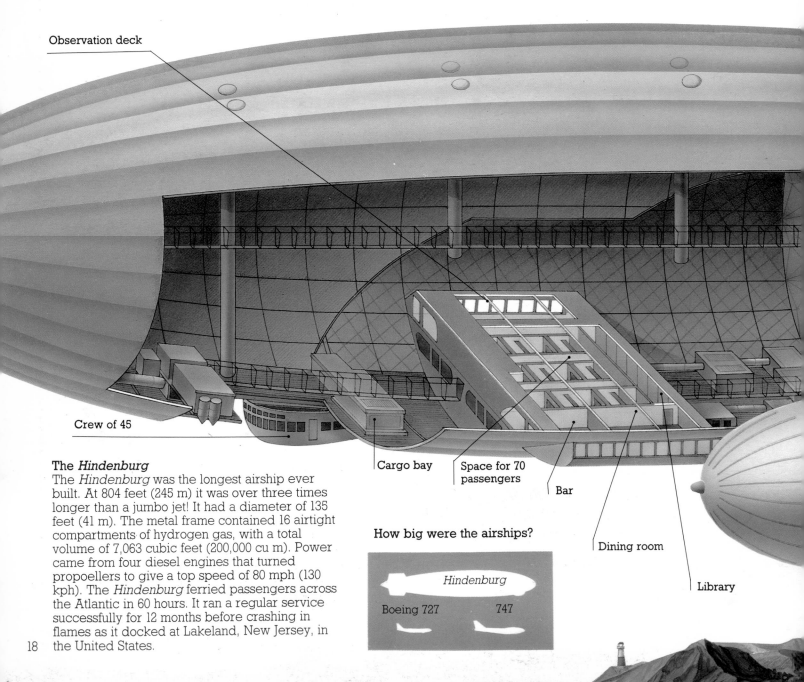

Observation deck

Crew of 45

Cargo bay

Space for 70 passengers

Bar

Dining room

Library

How big were the airships?

Hindenburg

Boeing 727   747

The *Hindenburg*

The *Hindenburg* was the longest airship ever built. At 804 feet (245 m) it was over three times longer than a jumbo jet! It had a diameter of 135 feet (41 m). The metal frame contained 16 airtight compartments of hydrogen gas, with a total volume of 7,063 cubic feet (200,000 cu m). Power came from four diesel engines that turned propoellers to give a top speed of 80 mph (130 kph). The *Hindenburg* ferried passengers across the Atlantic in 60 hours. It ran a regular service successfully for 12 months before crashing in flames as it docked at Lakeland, New Jersey, in the United States.

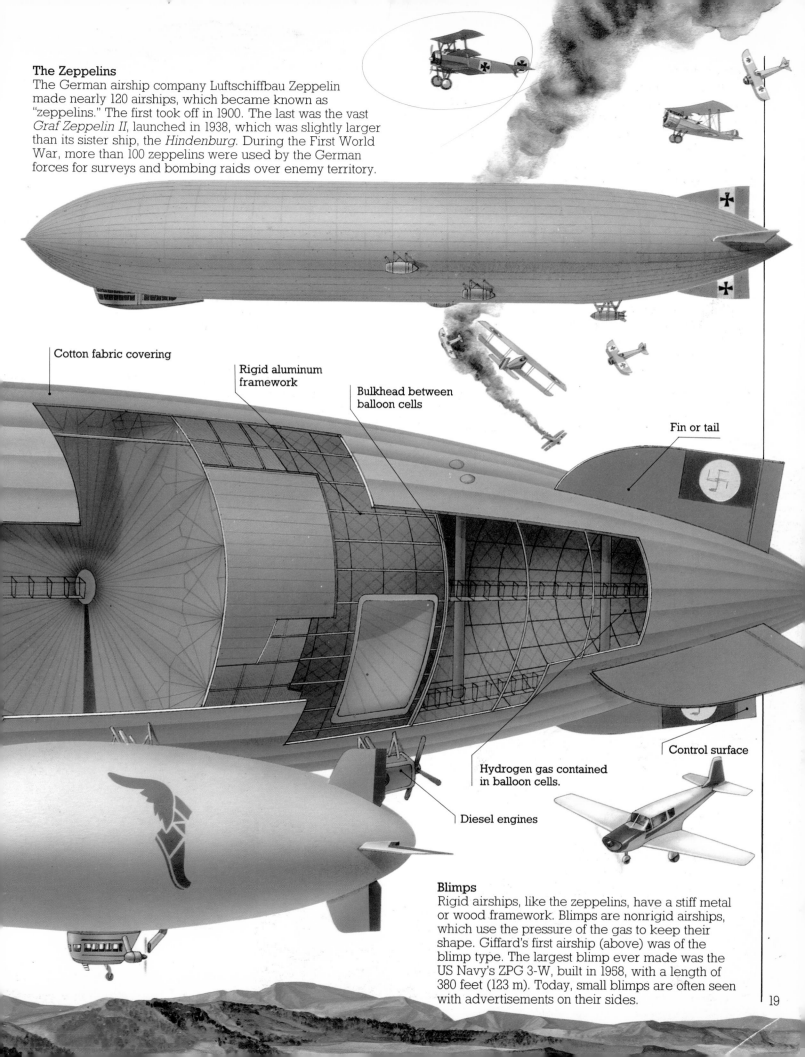

The Zeppelins

The German airship company Luftschiffbau Zeppelin made nearly 120 airships, which became known as "zeppelins." The first took off in 1900. The last was the vast *Graf Zeppelin II*, launched in 1938, which was slightly larger than its sister ship, the *Hindenburg*. During the First World War, more than 100 zeppelins were used by the German forces for surveys and bombing raids over enemy territory.

Cotton fabric covering

Rigid aluminum framework

Bulkhead between balloon cells

Fin or tail

Control surface

Hydrogen gas contained in balloon cells.

Diesel engines

Blimps

Rigid airships, like the zeppelins, have a stiff metal or wood framework. Blimps are nonrigid airships, which use the pressure of the gas to keep their shape. Giffard's first airship (above) was of the blimp type. The largest blimp ever made was the US Navy's ZPG 3-W, built in 1958, with a length of 380 feet (123 m). Today, small blimps are often seen with advertisements on their sides.

FLIGHT OF THE KITE

Kites are not true flying machines. They cannot stay up unless it is windy. Nor can they stay upwind of their controllers, they must float downwind. A typical kite has a strong but lightweight frame made of wood, metal, or plastic. This is covered by thin sheets of cloth, paper, or similar material. The kite is angled so that wind blows against its surface and pushes it both upward and downwind. One or more lines stop it blowing away and falling to the ground. Some designs need a tail to give stability and keep the kite in the right position relative to the wind.

The first kites were probably flown in the East thousands of years ago. They are still used in festivals and competitions, especially in Japan and China. The huge Japanese *o-dako* fighting kites have been flown for centuries. They are decorated with vivid pictures of warriors and controlled by up to 50 lines, worked by a dozen people. In the smaller one-line *nagasaki* fighting kites, the lines are coated with glue mixed with powdered glass, and contestants try to "saw" each other's kites free!

A festival of kites
Kite designs differ strikingly around the world. But they all need the energy of moving air, or wind, to push them upward. The record for the highest kite is over 25,000 feet (8,000 m), while the longest kite flight lasted for more than seven days.

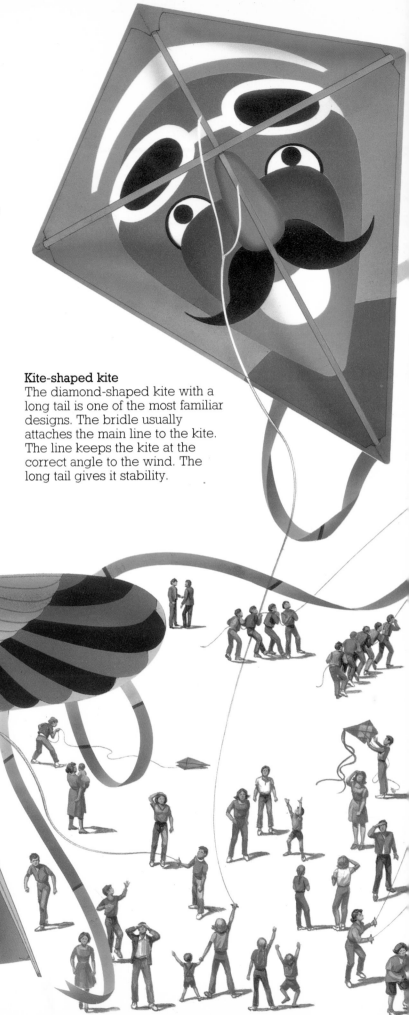

Kite-shaped kite
The diamond-shaped kite with a long tail is one of the most familiar designs. The bridle usually attaches the main line to the kite. The line keeps the kite at the correct angle to the wind. The long tail gives it stability.

Hawk kite
This kite has a long tail that keeps it steadily upright in the breeze. Some hawk kites are decorated to look like fierce-looking birds, with beaks and claws. Farmers fly these kites on automatic lines over their fields of crops. The silhouette of the hawk kite against the sky is supposed to frighten away seed-eating birds from the crops.

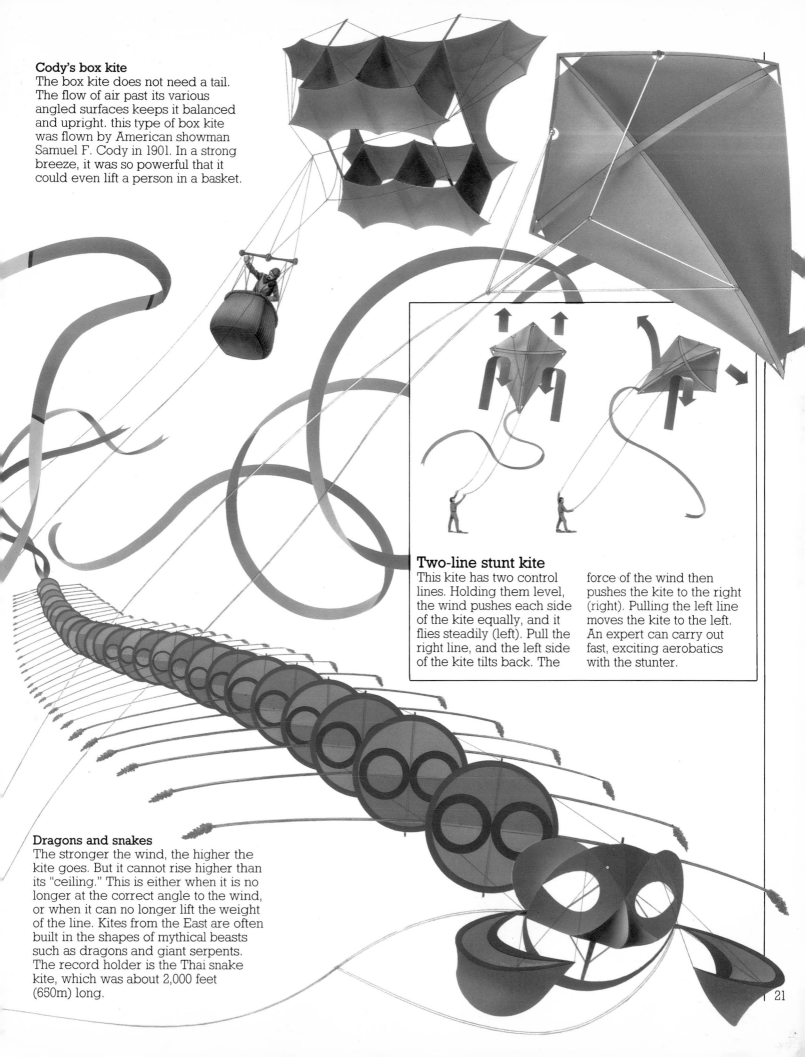

Cody's box kite

The box kite does not need a tail. The flow of air past its various angled surfaces keeps it balanced and upright. this type of box kite was flown by American showman Samuel F. Cody in 1901. In a strong breeze, it was so powerful that it could even lift a person in a basket.

Two-line stunt kite

This kite has two control lines. Holding them level, the wind pushes each side of the kite equally, and it flies steadily (left). Pull the right line, and the left side of the kite tilts back. The force of the wind then pushes the kite to the right (right). Pulling the left line moves the kite to the left. An expert can carry out fast, exciting aerobatics with the stunter.

Dragons and snakes

The stronger the wind, the higher the kite goes. But it cannot rise higher than its "ceiling." This is either when it is no longer at the correct angle to the wind, or when it can no longer lift the weight of the line. Kites from the East are often built in the shapes of mythical beasts such as dragons and giant serpents. The record holder is the Thai snake kite, which was about 2,000 feet (650m) long.

DROPPING IN

The parachute is not really a flying machine; it is more of a falling machine. The great Italian inventor and artist Leonardo da Vinci (page 12) sketched designs for parachutes in about 1495. Three centuries later, balloonist André-Jacques Garnerin made the world's first parachute drop over Paris, as he cut free his parachute and basket from a balloon.

Today, parachutes come in many sizes, designs, and styles. They are used to drop troops and supplies into difficult places. They slow down planes landing on aircraft carriers or short runways. In emergencies, they save the lives of pilots and passengers. They are also popular for "fun drops," and sport parachuting is exciting and competitive.

All parachutes work in the same basic way: as an air brake. The large area of the chute – about 323 square feet (30 sq m) in a modern steerable version – is greatly resisted by the air as it falls. The weight of the parachutist keeps the chute ballooned and opened out, to slow the descent. After the drop, the chute and its cords and lines are folded carefully into the pack, ready for next time.

Steerable parachute

The modern parachute is a great improvement on the simple umbrella-shaped design. It can be turned and steered by pulling on the cords. An expert parachutist can swoop down and land exactly on target.

The first parachutist

In 1783, French doctor Sebastien Lenormand jumped from a tower and floated down on a parasollike device. But the first true parachute descent from mid-air was by another Frenchman, André-Jacques Garnerin, four years later. He floated down from a height of about 3,270 feet (1,000 m) and landed without injury.

Garnerin made hundreds of drops over the following years.

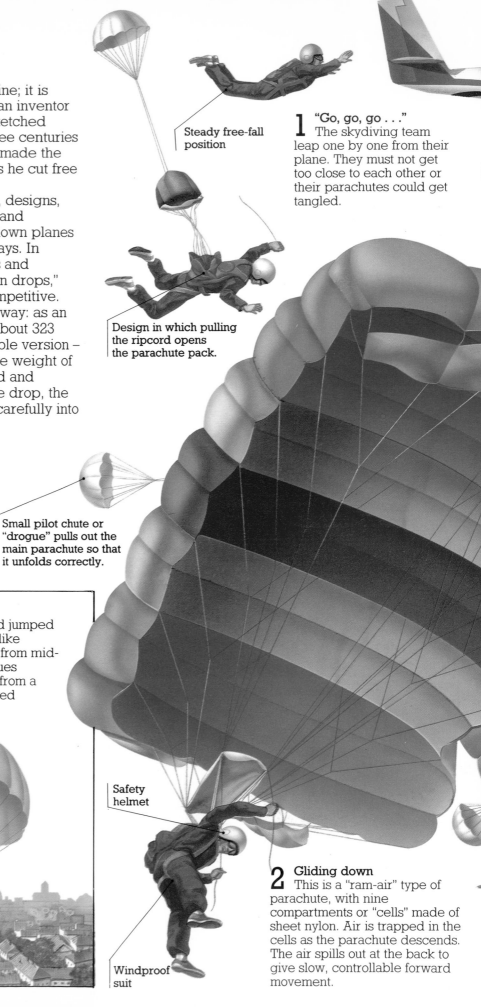

Steady free-fall position

Design in which pulling the ripcord opens the parachute pack.

Small pilot chute or "drogue" pulls out the main parachute so that it unfolds correctly.

Safety helmet

Windproof suit

1 "Go, go, go . . ."
The skydiving team leap one by one from their plane. They must not get too close to each other or their parachutes could get tangled.

2 Gliding down
This is a "ram-air" type of parachute, with nine compartments or "cells" made of sheet nylon. Air is trapped in the cells as the parachute descends. The air spills out at the back to give slow, controllable forward movement.

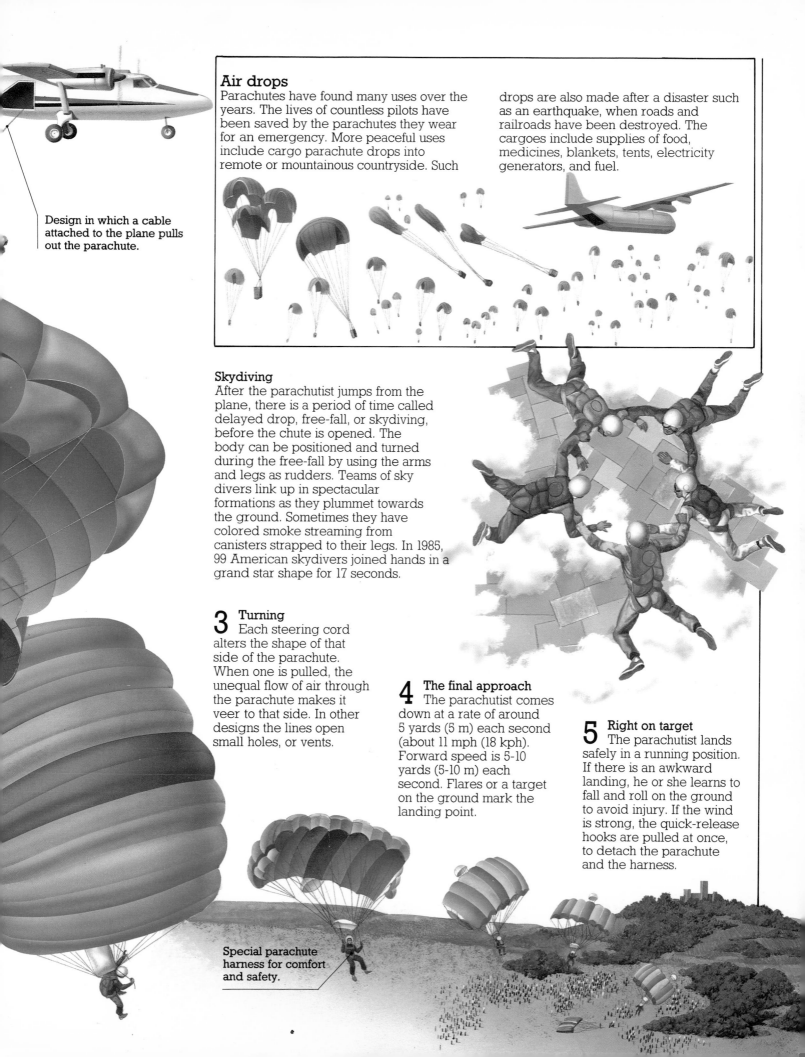

Design in which a cable attached to the plane pulls out the parachute.

Air drops

Parachutes have found many uses over the years. The lives of countless pilots have been saved by the parachutes they wear for an emergency. More peaceful uses include cargo parachute drops into remote or mountainous countryside. Such drops are also made after a disaster such as an earthquake, when roads and railroads have been destroyed. The cargoes include supplies of food, medicines, blankets, tents, electricity generators, and fuel.

Skydiving

After the parachutist jumps from the plane, there is a period of time called delayed drop, free-fall, or skydiving, before the chute is opened. The body can be positioned and turned during the free-fall by using the arms and legs as rudders. Teams of sky divers link up in spectacular formations as they plummet towards the ground. Sometimes they have colored smoke streaming from canisters strapped to their legs. In 1985, 99 American skydivers joined hands in a grand star shape for 17 seconds.

3 Turning
Each steering cord alters the shape of that side of the parachute. When one is pulled, the unequal flow of air through the parachute makes it veer to that side. In other designs the lines open small holes, or vents.

4 The final approach
The parachutist comes down at a rate of around 5 yards (5 m) each second (about 11 mph (18 kph). Forward speed is 5-10 yards (5-10 m) each second. Flares or a target on the ground mark the landing point.

5 Right on target
The parachutist lands safely in a running position. If there is an awkward landing, he or she learns to fall and roll on the ground to avoid injury. If the wind is strong, the quick-release hooks are pulled at once, to detach the parachute and the harness.

Special parachute harness for comfort and safety.

RIDING THE AIR

In 1889, the German aero pioneer Otto Lilienthal published his book *Bird Flight as the Basis for Aviation*. Lilienthal had read about the work of Sir George Cayley (page 26), and spent many years studying the way birds fly, soar, and glide. In 1891, Lilienthal flew in his first glider. His design was of the hang-glider type, where the pilot hangs from the gliding wing. In this arrangement, the body weight below the wing gives the craft stability, in the same way as the tail that hangs from a kite. Lilienthal even had his own hill made, near Berlin, so that he could test and improve his gliders.

In the 1970s, new types of hang gliders were developed. Their wing design is based on a type of "parachute glider," known as the Rogallo wing, which was developed by Professor Francis Rogallo in the United States during the 1950s. Rogallo's wing was intended to carry space capsules back to Earth. Since then, hang gliders have become very popular. This is partly because they can be taken to pieces and packed for travel by car. They can also be flown wherever a good breeze blows against a slope or cliff, or where a winch or car can tow the glider into the air.

Hanging around
A modern hang glider is made of advanced lightweight materials such as aluminum alloys and carbon fibers. The pilot steers by shifting his or her body weight. The longest hang glide is over 175 miles (300 km) and the highest altitude reached is 14,225 feet (4,343 m).

Wing spar
The main spar at the front gives the wing shape, stiffness, and the correct curve. As in Lilienthal's "gliding machine," it is secured by guy lines above and below.

Rib battens
Stiff strips slot into channels along the wing. They help give the correct aerofoil shape to the wing, which improves its lifting power.

Wing panel
The wing material is usually a special type of sheet nylon or plastic. It is extremely light yet strong, airtight, and tear resistant. After a flight it must be folded carefully so that it does not harden and crack during storage.

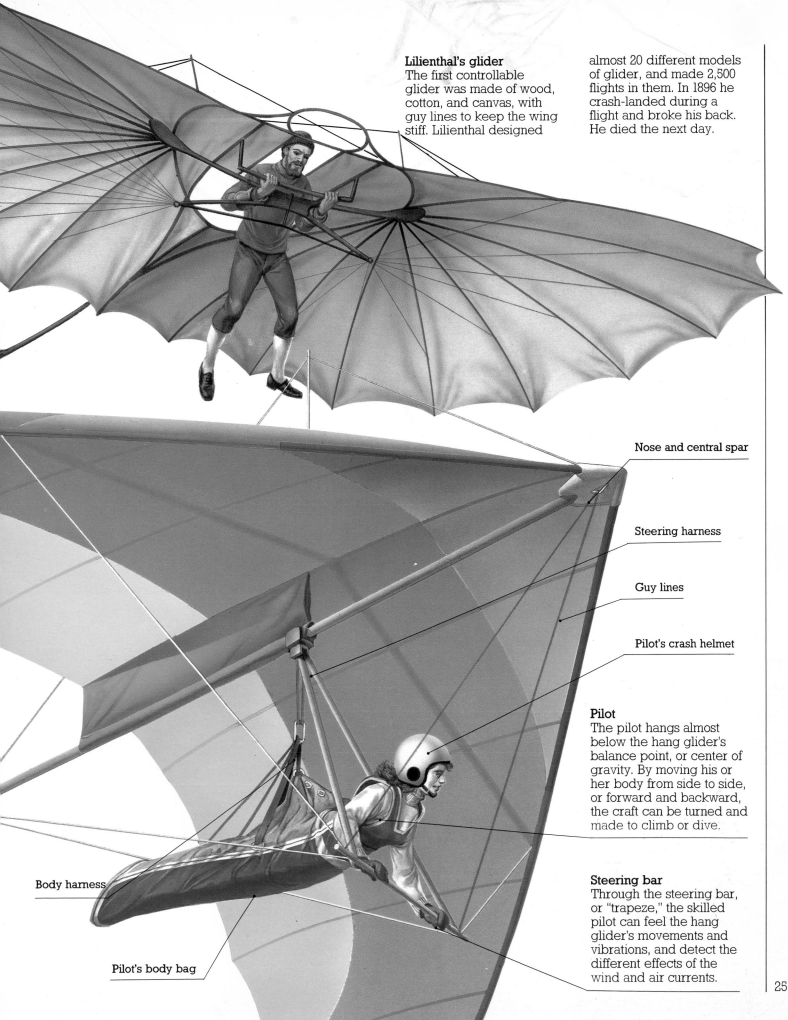

Lilienthal's glider
The first controllable glider was made of wood, cotton, and canvas, with guy lines to keep the wing stiff. Lilienthal designed almost 20 different models of glider, and made 2,500 flights in them. In 1896 he crash-landed during a flight and broke his back. He died the next day.

Nose and central spar

Steering harness

Guy lines

Pilot's crash helmet

Pilot
The pilot hangs almost below the hang glider's balance point, or center of gravity. By moving his or her body from side to side, or forward and backward, the craft can be turned and made to climb or dive.

Body harness

Steering bar
Through the steering bar, or "trapeze," the skilled pilot can feel the hang glider's movements and vibrations, and detect the different effects of the wind and air currents.

Pilot's body bag

25

SOARING LIKE A BIRD

Gliding has been called the "purest way to fly." The glider, or sailplane, has no engine. It relies entirely on efficient design and pilot skill to stay up. A typical competition glider has a wingspan of 49 feet (15 m) and weighs less than 1,102 pounds (500 kg). It can become airborne in several ways. It may be towed up on a cable by a towplane. Or it can be hoisted like a kite on a long cable, which is wound at high speed on to a winch or towed behind a car. In still air, the modern glider comes down with a glide ratio of about 40. This means that for every 131 feet (40 m) it travels forward, it drops 3 feet (1 m) downward. However, not all air is still. Where wind blows against a slope or bluff, the air is forced upward and forms an updraft. Or, in certain conditions, the Sun heats up the ground quickly, the ground warms the air above, and this air rises as a thermal. If the pilot can fly into the rising air, the glider will be carried upward, too. In good conditions, a glider can fly for as long as the pilot stays alert.

The spindly sailplane

A glider is designed to cope with the stresses of flying. On the ground, it looks weak and fragile – and it is. Push the wrong part, and it could snap off. The craft's shape is as smooth and streamlined as possible, to give aerodynamic efficiency.

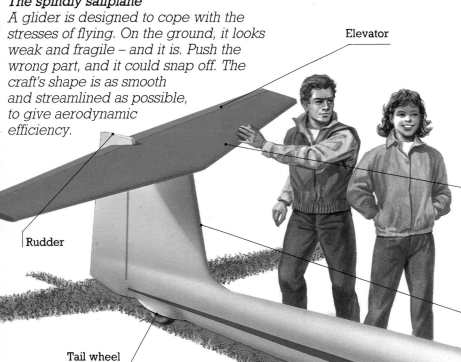

Elevator

Rudder

Tail wheel

Tailplane
The small back or "stabilizer" wing is known as the tailplane. In steady flight, it keeps the main wing at the proper angle to the airflow. The control surfaces of the tailplane, known as elevators, pitch the craft's nose up or down.

Fin
This is the correct name for the "tail." With the tailplane, it gives stability and helps stop the back part of the glider swinging around. Its control surface is called the rudder, which turns the glider to the left or right.

Cayley's contraption

In the 1800s, the Englishman Sir George Cayley drew designs for many gliding machines, though few were built. In 1853, one of his grand-daughters said that she did not believe his machines would fly. So Cayley had a full-sized version built, ordered his coach driver to get in, and launched it from a hill in Yorkshire. The craft flew about 1,640 feet (500 m) before crashlanding. The frightened driver wanted to resign at once. Even so, he was the world's first glider pilot.

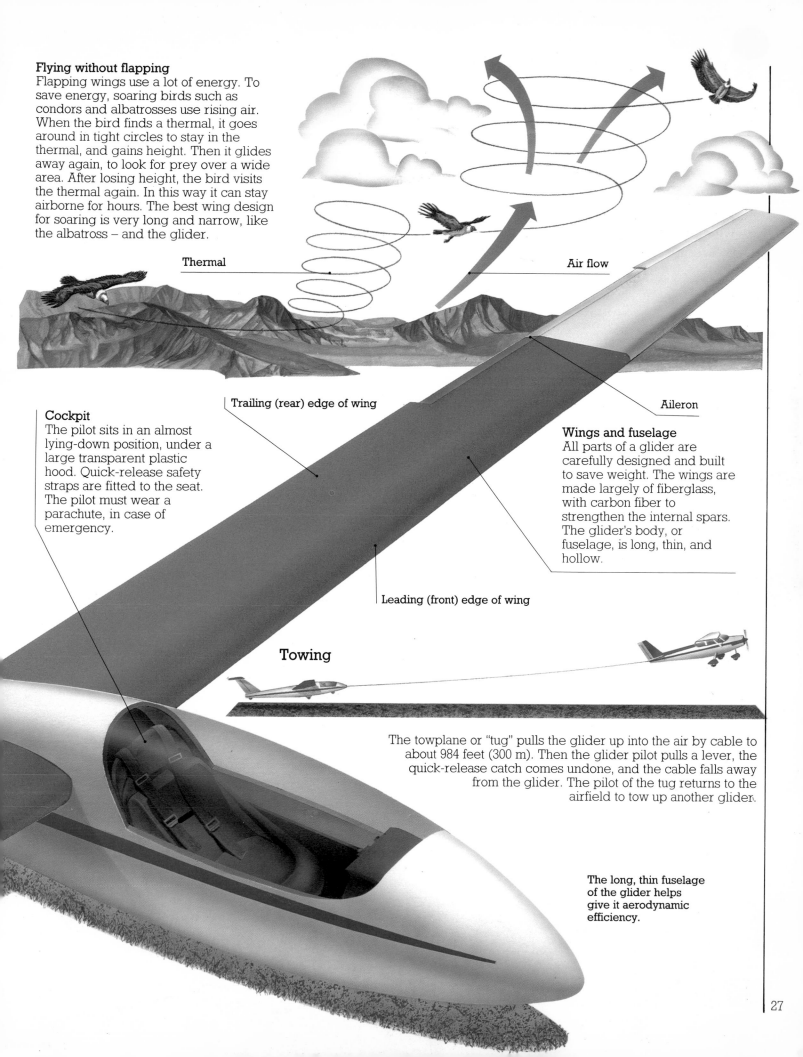

Flying without flapping

Flapping wings use a lot of energy. To save energy, soaring birds such as condors and albatrosses use rising air. When the bird finds a thermal, it goes around in tight circles to stay in the thermal, and gains height. Then it glides away again, to look for prey over a wide area. After losing height, the bird visits the thermal again. In this way it can stay airborne for hours. The best wing design for soaring is very long and narrow, like the albatross – and the glider.

Thermal

Air flow

Trailing (rear) edge of wing

Aileron

Cockpit

The pilot sits in an almost lying-down position, under a large transparent plastic hood. Quick-release safety straps are fitted to the seat. The pilot must wear a parachute, in case of emergency.

Wings and fuselage

All parts of a glider are carefully designed and built to save weight. The wings are made largely of fiberglass, with carbon fiber to strengthen the internal spars. The glider's body, or fuselage, is long, thin, and hollow.

Leading (front) edge of wing

Towing

The towplane or "tug" pulls the glider up into the air by cable to about 984 feet (300 m). Then the glider pilot pulls a lever, the quick-release catch comes undone, and the cable falls away from the glider. The pilot of the tug returns to the airfield to tow up another glider.

The long, thin fuselage of the glider helps give it aerodynamic efficiency.

THE WRIGHT *FLYER*

By the beginning of this century, people had flown in balloons, airships, parachutes, and gliders. But no one had built a heavier-than-air flying machine that could travel under its own power and go where the pilot wished – a true airplane. However, in the United States, two brothers, Orville and Wilbur Wright, were laying plans. The brothers had a bicycle-making business in Dayton, Ohio, and worked in a scientific, step-by-step way, using their skills as engineers.

The Wrights first experimented with kites and gliders, continuing the progress made by pioneers such as Otto Lilienthal and Octave Chanute. They found a suitable beach on America's East coast, with a steady and predictable wind. After dozens of glider flights there in 1902, they were ready to make the first airplane flight. The Wrights knew that steam engines were too heavy for their purpose. Even gasoline engines, at that time being developed for the early cars, were not light enough. So they designed and built their own small engine. In 1903, it powered the Wright *Flyer* for the world's first airplane flight.

A bird's-eye view of the *Flyer*
The time: 10.35 am on Thursday, December 17, 1903. The place: an isolated, windswept beach near Kitty Hawk, North Carolina, the United States. The Wright Flyer *moves along its track and lifts into the air, with Orville at the controls. The flight lasted only 12 seconds and covered a distance of just 121 feet (37 m). But it was the first successful trip in a self-propelled, heavier-than-air flying machine.*

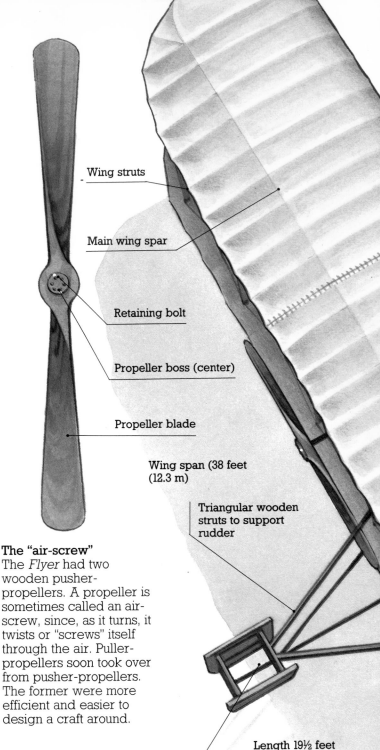

Wing struts

Main wing spar

Retaining bolt

Propeller boss (center)

Propeller blade

Wing span (38 feet (12.3 m)

Triangular wooden struts to support rudder

Length 19½ feet (6.4 m)

The "air-screw"
The *Flyer* had two wooden pusher-propellers. A propeller is sometimes called an air-screw, since, as it turns, it twists or "screws" itself through the air. Puller-propellers soon took over from pusher-propellers. The former were more efficient and easier to design a craft around.

Track rails
Wheels or skids would have become stuck in the sand of the North Carolina beach. So the Wrights constructed a two-railed track, like a miniature railway line. The *Flyer* rolled along this on a small wheeled trolly as it gathered speed for takeoff.

Independent observers, newspaper reporter, and official photographer

Wheeled trolley

Two-railed track

Rudders
Two rudders at the back of the *Flyer* prevented the craft swinging from side to side. The design of the plane's control surfaces, such as these rudders, had been carefully tested on gliders and on models in the Wrights' specially built wind tunnel.

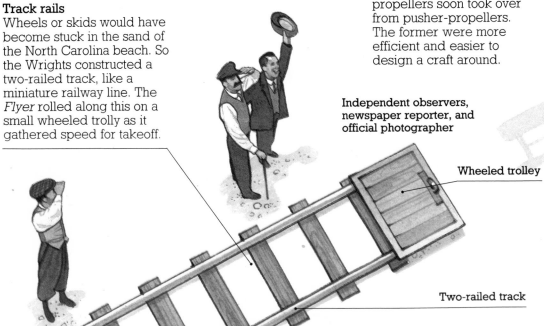

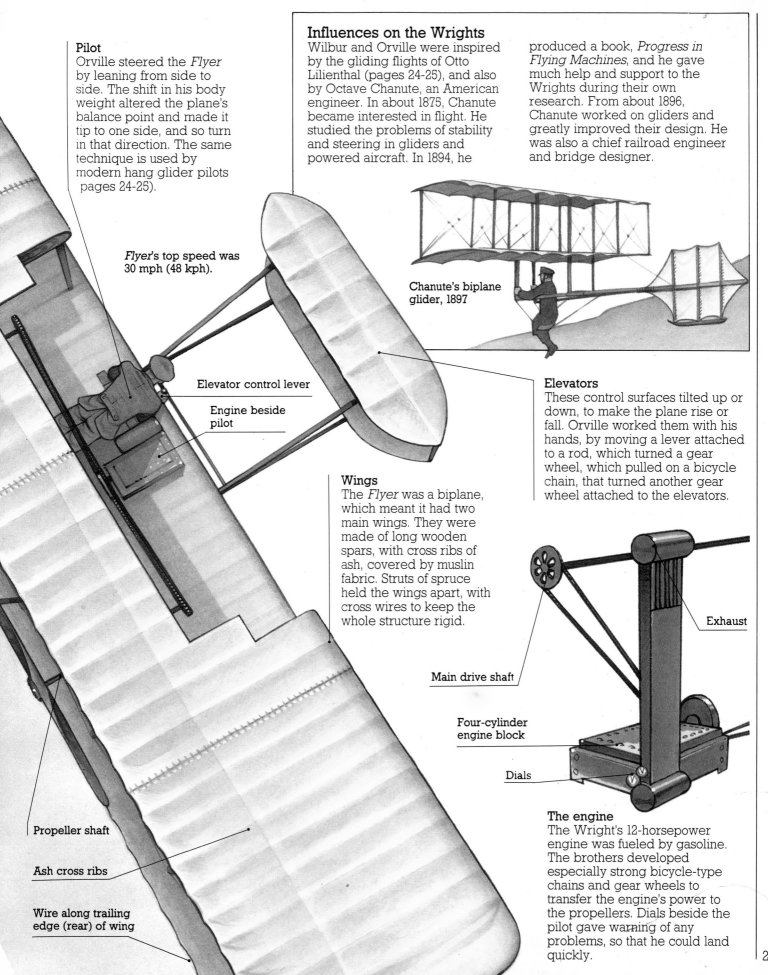

Pilot
Orville steered the *Flyer* by leaning from side to side. The shift in his body weight altered the plane's balance point and made it tip to one side, and so turn in that direction. The same technique is used by modern hang glider pilots (pages 24-25).

Flyer's top speed was 30 mph (48 kph).

Elevator control lever

Engine beside pilot

Influences on the Wrights
Wilbur and Orville were inspired by the gliding flights of Otto Lilienthal (pages 24-25), and also by Octave Chanute, an American engineer. In about 1875, Chanute became interested in flight. He studied the problems of stability and steering in gliders and powered aircraft. In 1894, he produced a book, *Progress in Flying Machines*, and he gave much help and support to the Wrights during their own research. From about 1896, Chanute worked on gliders and greatly improved their design. He was also a chief railroad engineer and bridge designer.

Chanute's biplane glider, 1897

Elevators
These control surfaces tilted up or down, to make the plane rise or fall. Orville worked them with his hands, by moving a lever attached to a rod, which turned a gear wheel, which pulled on a bicycle chain, that turned another gear wheel attached to the elevators.

Wings
The *Flyer* was a biplane, which meant it had two main wings. They were made of long wooden spars, with cross ribs of ash, covered by muslin fabric. Struts of spruce held the wings apart, with cross wires to keep the whole structure rigid.

Exhaust

Main drive shaft

Four-cylinder engine block

Dials

Propeller shaft

Ash cross ribs

Wire along trailing edge (rear) of wing

The engine
The Wright's 12-horsepower engine was fueled by gasoline. The brothers developed especially strong bicycle-type chains and gear wheels to transfer the engine's power to the propellers. Dials beside the pilot gave warning of any problems, so that he could land quickly.

29

FLYING FIRST AND FAMOUS FLYERS

The Wright brothers made the first airplane flight in 1903. Since then, many pilots and planes have won their places in the history books. One of the earliest challenges was to be first across natural obstacles, such as oceans and mountains. There were also ever-increasing speed and distance records.

The first Atlantic crossing by plane was by Lieutenant Read and his team in May 1919, in American NC-4 flying boats. They stopped in the Azores to refuel, and the trip took 11 days. The first nonstop Atlantic flight was a month later, by John Alcock and Arthur Brown, taking 16 hours. The first nonstop Atlantic solo flight was not until eight years later, by Charles Lindberg. The year after this, Charles Smith and three colleagues flew over the Pacific. They took off from California and flew to Brisbane. During the 1930s, many flying records were set. The first solo round-the-world flight was by Wiley Post, an American, in 1933. He took nearly eight days, refueling at stops along the way.

Blériot XI

The first cross Channel flight was by Frenchman Louis Blériot, on July 25, 1909. His *Blériot XI* flew 23 miles (37 kms) from France to England at 45 mph (72 kph), and landed near Dover. Blériot won a prize of £1,000 from a London newspaper.

Fokker Triplane

The German "Red Baron," Manfred von Richthofen, was probably the greatest fighter pilot of World War One. He shot down 80 enemy planes, many from his three-winged Fokker Triplane, as he twisted and turned in "dogfights" over the trenches.

Sopwith Camel

The British Camels were deadly opponents of the German Fokkers during World War One. About 5,500 Camels were made, and they destroyed nearly 1,300 enemy aircraft. The name comes from the humplike cover over the machine guns.

Vickers Vimy

The first nonstop flight across the Atlantic was on July 14-15, 1919. Pilot John Alcock and navigator Arthur Brown flew a twin-engined Vickers Vimy from St. John's, Newfoundland, to western Ireland. The Vimy was converted to hold extra fuel instead of weapons.

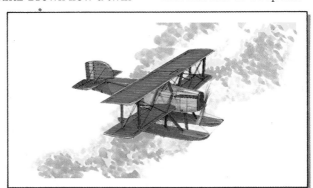

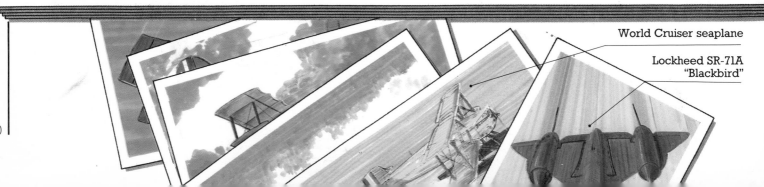

World Cruiser seaplane

Lockheed SR-71A "Blackbird"

Stops and starts
Improvements in aircraft speed and design have happened in "jumps." Many advances were made during wartime, as each side tried to build planes that flew faster and farther, higher or lower, and with better weapons. During World War One, planes developed from flimsy and unsafe "stringbags" to speedy and maneuvrable fighters such as the Fokker Triplane and Camel, in just four years.

Spirit of St. Louis
The first nonstop solo flight across the Atlantic was by Charles Lindberg, on May 20-21, 1927. He used a specially built Ryan M2 monoplane, which he named *Spirit of St. Louis*. It carried 506 gallons (2,300 l) of fuel and took more than 33 hours.

"Flying Fortress"
The US Air Force B-17 "Flying Fortress" was a World War Two bomber with a wing span of 1,036 feet (31.6 m). It bristled with machine guns and could carry nearly three tons (2,700 kg) of bombs. Fortresses carried out many raids over Germany.

Stars of show and screen
In the period between World Wars One and Two, aircraft became much safer and more reliable. They and their pilots soon became stars in spectacular stunts at air shows and in the movies. "Wing-walking" was an exciting event when people stood, walked, and even danced in midair.

Hawker Hurricane
The Hurricane had a top speed of 320 mph (520 kph). It entered service in 1937 and was one of the most successful fighter planes in World War Two. Royal Air Force pilots flew hundreds of Hurricanes, as well as Spitfires, to defend their country in the Battle of Britain against the German Luftwaffe in 1940.

Flying Fortress

Cessna A-37 Thunderbolt

LIGHT AIRCRAFT

The small, propeller-driven "light aircraft" is the most popular type of plane in the air today. It can be used for many tasks, ranging from crop spraying to the emergency airlift of an ill patient.

The light plane has all the main parts of any aircraft. Its chief structures are the fuselage, wings, tailplane, and fin, which together are known as the airframe. The engine at the front provides the driving power. The smaller parts are divided into systems, to help in design, building, and maintenance. In a light plane, these systems are relatively small and simple. In a jetliner such as the Airbus (page 40) there are yards of electrical cables and many miles of hydraulic piping!

Fin
The fin, sometimes called the "tail," is fixed firmly to the fuselage at the back. It prevents the back of the plane swinging from side to side. Attached to the fin by hinges is a control surface, known as the rudder (page 34).

Rudder

Fuselage 23 feet (7 m) long

Elevator

Tailplane

Parts of a plane
The Piper Cherokee is a well-known and much used small plane. In areas like North America and Australia, where people regularly travel long distances, planes such as the Cherokee are used almost like family cars. An air trip is virtually an everyday occurence.

Control cables
Strong metal cables run from the pilot's control stick and rudder pedals to the control surfaces. The cables are led around pulleys and through slots in the plane's framework. As the pilot moves the controls, these pull the cables, which in turn pull on the surfaces and move them.

Crosswinds
Imagine swimming across a river. You would be carried downstream by the current, so you would have to aim slightly upstream to reach the bank opposite. In the same way, a pilot must allow for wind strength and direction. A crosswind, which blows from the side, pushes the plane sideways. So the pilot must aim slightly upwind of where he or she wishes to go.

Wing
The wing gets its strength from long rods or girders called spars, which stretch from the fuselage to the wing tip. The ribs are curved pieces of metal that give the wing its aerofoil shape when seen from the side (page 35).

Flap

Plane points in this direction (slightly west of north).

Plane flies in this direction (slightly east of north).

Wind blows from west to east.

N
W E
S

Compass

Plane starts here.

Wing covered by thin aluminum sheeting.

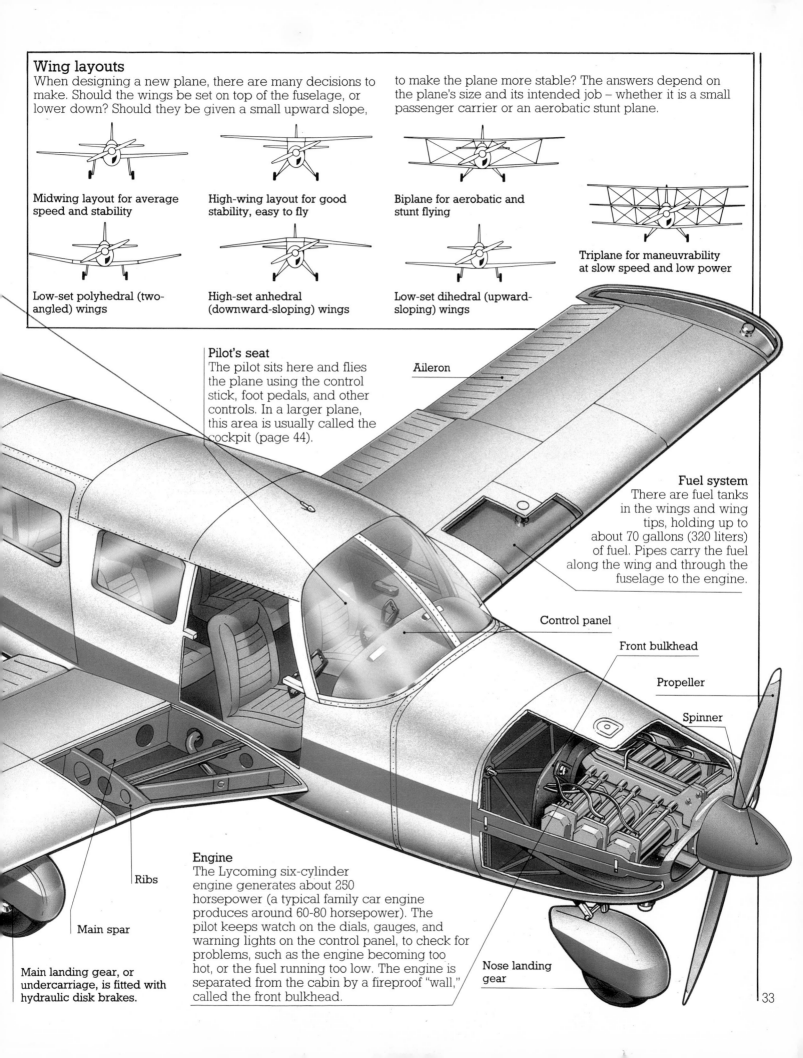

Wing layouts

When designing a new plane, there are many decisions to make. Should the wings be set on top of the fuselage, or lower down? Should they be given a small upward slope, to make the plane more stable? The answers depend on the plane's size and its intended job – whether it is a small passenger carrier or an aerobatic stunt plane.

Midwing layout for average speed and stability

High-wing layout for good stability, easy to fly

Biplane for aerobatic and stunt flying

Triplane for maneuvrability at slow speed and low power

Low-set polyhedral (two-angled) wings

High-set anhedral (downward-sloping) wings

Low-set dihedral (upward-sloping) wings

Pilot's seat
The pilot sits here and flies the plane using the control stick, foot pedals, and other controls. In a larger plane, this area is usually called the cockpit (page 44).

Aileron

Fuel system
There are fuel tanks in the wings and wing tips, holding up to about 70 gallons (320 liters) of fuel. Pipes carry the fuel along the wing and through the fuselage to the engine.

Control panel

Front bulkhead

Propeller

Spinner

Ribs

Main spar

Main landing gear, or undercarriage, is fitted with hydraulic disk brakes.

Engine
The Lycoming six-cylinder engine generates about 250 horsepower (a typical family car engine produces around 60-80 horsepower). The pilot keeps watch on the dials, gauges, and warning lights on the control panel, to check for problems, such as the engine becoming too hot, or the fuel running too low. The engine is separated from the cabin by a fireproof "wall," called the front bulkhead.

Nose landing gear

CONTROL IN THE AIR

A typical aircraft is guided and steered by three main sets of control surfaces: a rudder on the fin, two elevators on the tailplane, and two ailerons on the wings. These work on the basic scientific principle of "action and reaction."

As the plane flies straight and level, air flows smoothly past it. When one of the control surfaces is tilted into the airstream, the air rushing past pushes against it. This is the "action." The control surface responds by moving away, and pulling that part of the plane with it. This is the "reaction."

The other main controls of an aircraft are the throttles. These adjust the amounts of fuel and air being fed into the engines. This in turn makes them speed up or slow down, which alters the speed of the plane.

Up, around, and back down
A new pilot is learning to fly this Canadair CL-215 general purpose transport plane. The pilot gets used to the controls and the craft's handling by flying "circuits." A circuit involves all the main aerial maneuvres: taking off, climbing, banking and turning, and descending, before landing back on the same runway.

Turning
In order to turn to the right, the pilot steers the control column in that direction. This moves the rudder control surface on the fin to the right, which pushes the plane's back end to the left – this in turn means the front swings around to the right.

Left aileron tilts downward.

Rudder swings to right.

Elevators tilt upward to make plane ascend.

Leaving the runway
By the time the Canadair has traveled about 700 yards (650 m) it has reached take off speed of 150 mph (250 kph). The pilot pulls back the control column, which tilts the elevator control surfaces upward. The plane rises into the air.

Ready for takeoff
The Canadair waits at the end of the runway, wheel brakes on and engines ticking over. The air traffic controller in the airport control tower gives the all clear over the radio. The pilot opens the throttles for full power from the engines. The brakes are released, and the plane begins its takeoff.

Wing is more curved on the upper surface than on the lower surface (aerofoil section).

Low air pressure above wing gives "lift" and sucks wind upward.

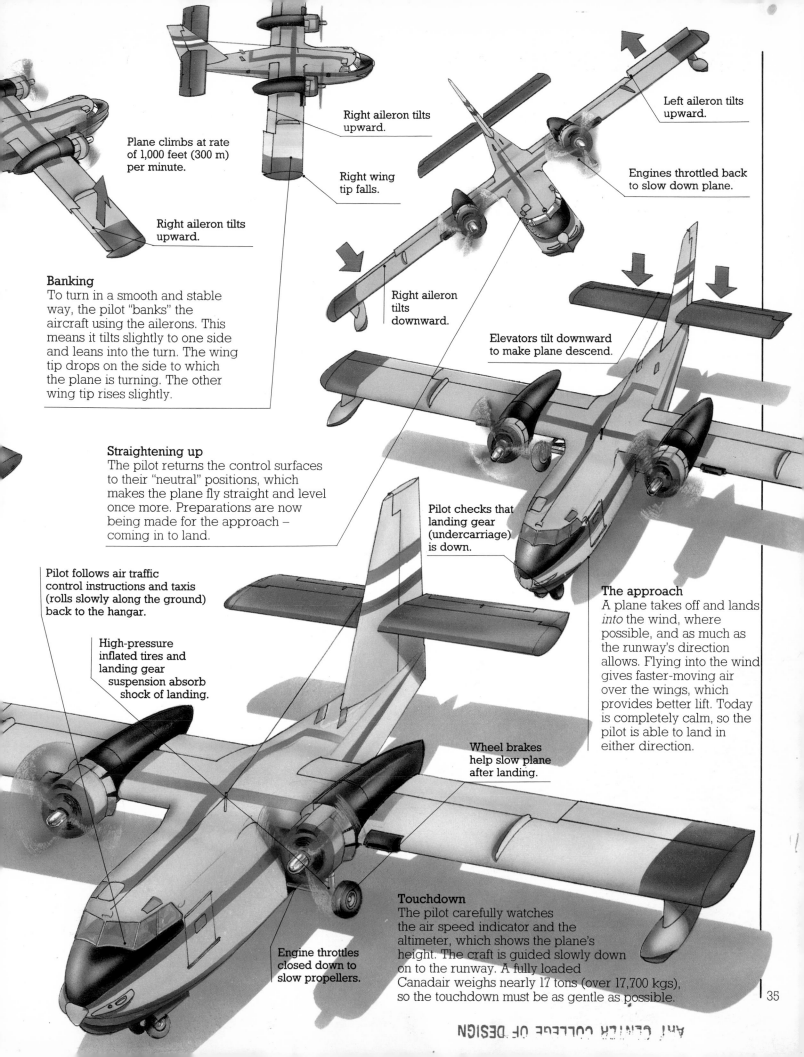

Plane climbs at rate of 1,000 feet (300 m) per minute.

Right aileron tilts upward.

Right wing tip falls.

Right aileron tilts upward.

Left aileron tilts upward.

Engines throttled back to slow down plane.

Right aileron tilts downward.

Elevators tilt downward to make plane descend.

Banking
To turn in a smooth and stable way, the pilot "banks" the aircraft using the ailerons. This means it tilts slightly to one side and leans into the turn. The wing tip drops on the side to which the plane is turning. The other wing tip rises slightly.

Straightening up
The pilot returns the control surfaces to their "neutral" positions, which makes the plane fly straight and level once more. Preparations are now being made for the approach – coming in to land.

Pilot follows air traffic control instructions and taxis (rolls slowly along the ground) back to the hangar.

High-pressure inflated tires and landing gear suspension absorb shock of landing.

Pilot checks that landing gear (undercarriage) is down.

The approach
A plane takes off and lands *into* the wind, where possible, and as much as the runway's direction allows. Flying into the wind gives faster-moving air over the wings, which provides better lift. Today is completely calm, so the pilot is able to land in either direction.

Wheel brakes help slow plane after landing.

Touchdown
The pilot carefully watches the air speed indicator and the altimeter, which shows the plane's height. The craft is guided slowly down on to the runway. A fully loaded Canadair weighs nearly 17 tons (over 17,700 kgs), so the touchdown must be as gentle as possible.

Engine throttles closed down to slow propellers.

FIRE FIGHTER IN THE SKY

Aircraft are expensive to buy and run. A general transport and utility plane like the Canadair CL-215 uses over 170 U.S. gallons (650 liters) of fuel *every hour*. (This is almost 100 times the amount of fuel used by a family car.) An engine overhaul, needed after 1,500 hours of running time, costs more than $100,000. And this particular plane is noted for being very economical to run! Even so, such amounts become very small when compared to the money lost in a burned-out warehouse of electronic equipment, or a smoldering forest of valuable timber trees. For this reason, specially equipped fire fighting planes are sometimes used to "water bomb" big blazes.

Chemical blanket

The Canadair carries a special tank of fire fighting foam chemical, a little of which is added to each load of water. As the water falls on to the flames, the chemical turns it into a foam that is more than twice as effective at putting out flames as water would be alone.

Dousing the flames

A Canadair CL-215 has been called in to fight a forest fire that could destroy millions of dollars worth of timber. A nearby lake is the source of water. The plane lands on the lake, scoops water into its internal tanks, takes off, and drops the water over the burning trees in the form of a heavy rain.

The approach

This Canadair has two special fire fighting tanks in the fuselage, which together hold 1,400 U.S. gallons (almost 5,350 liters) of water. As the plane approaches the lake, two scooping pipes are lowered under the fuselage.

Wing floats prevent wing tips dipping into water in rough conditions.

The scoop

A fire fighter like the Canadair is able to reach the scene of a fire quickly, especially if it is a remote forest, and catch the fire before it spreads too far. As the plane's boat-shaped fuselage skims along the surface, water is forced up the scooping pipes into the tanks. A normal scooping run is about 1,700 feet (550 m) long at a speed of 80 mph (130 kph). Including the landing and take off, the plane needs some 4,000 feet (1,200 m) of clear water.

All-around visibility from large front windows helps pilot to judge the aim.

Chemical tank in fuselage

Preparing to drop

To release the water, the pilot presses a switch on the control column. This opens the doors that form part of the floor of the water tanks. Flying slowly, at around 110 mph (175 kph), and at a height of only 150 feet (45m), the drop can be aimed with great accuracy. In a double drop, both sets of doors open together and dump the full load of water.

The douse

The water begins to quench the fire and bring it under control. The pilot then returns to the lake to refill the tanks. The plane can make over 30 drops in the four-hour period before its fuel starts to run low.

Skimming the surface

The skimmer is a bird that catches its food by swooping low over the water's surface, with the bottom part of its bill dipped into the water. As soon as it touches a small fish or similar water creature, the skimmer snaps its bill shut and jerks the prey clear of the water.

Skimmer has a wing span of over 2 feet (60 cm).

JET POWER

During the 1930s, British pilot and aero engineer Frank Whittle worked on ideas for jet propulsion. Instead of a twirling propeller that pulled the aircraft along, hot gases rushing from the back of a jet engine would push it along. But Whittle's designs did not attract much money or support. He had to work with a small team, often in his spare time, in a shed. In 1937 the world's first jet engine was started up, fixed firmly to Whittle's test bench.

One of the German designers, Hans von Ohain, borrowed ideas from Whittle and tested his own engine a few months later. Then, in 1939, the first jet-powered aircraft roared into the sky. It was a German Heinkel He-178. Since that time, jet engines have become bigger, more powerful, and more economical with fuel. But they still work in the same way as Whittle's early designs. Air is sucked into the front of the engine and squeezed under great pressure by the spinning blades of a compressor. It is then sprayed with fuel and set on fire. The hot jet gases blast backward out of the engine, pushing it forward.

Inside the turbofan jet

Most modern airliners are powered by turbofan jet engines. The turbofan has a very large, many-bladed turbine, like an enormous electric fan, at the front. This is called the intake fan. It blows most of the air through the outer part of the engine casing, around the central engine. This cooler air flows over the hot casing of the central engine and stops it becoming too hot.

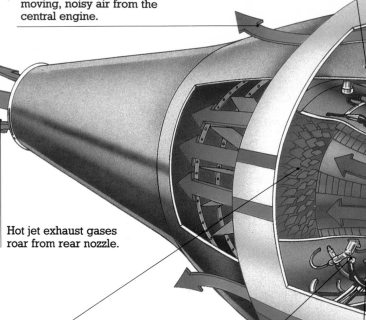

Air blown through outer casing comes out here and surrounds the hot, fast-moving, noisy air from the central engine.

Central part of engine casing

Hot jet exhaust gases roar from rear nozzle.

Fuel pipes

6 Turbines
As the burning gases rush out of the combustion chamber, they make these turbines spin around with great force. The turbines, which are made of heat-resistant materials, are fastened to the main drive shaft, making it turn, too.

5 Combustion chamber
Jet fuel (kerosene) is sprayed into the compressed air in this special heat-resistant chamber. The fuel and air burn in a sort of continuous and controlled "slow explosion."

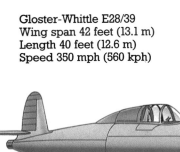

Gloster-Whittle E28/39
Wing span 42 feet (13.1 m)
Length 40 feet (12.6 m)
Speed 350 mph (560 kph)

Boeing 707
Wing span 146 feet (44.5 m)
Length 153 feet (46.6 m)
Speed 534 mph (860 kph)

Gloster-Whittle E28/39

The E28/39 was one of the first jet planes. It was powered by a turbojet designed by Frank Whittle. During World War Two, Germany also developed jets. In 1944 the first jet planes to enter air battles were German Messerschmitt Me 262s. With a top speed of over 500 mph (800 kph) they were faster than other fighters, but they came into the war too late.

Boeing 707

In 1949, the world's first jetliner took to the air. It was the de Havilland Comet, which could carry 36 passengers at 455 mph (730 kph). By 1952, it was flying regular passenger services. In 1954, the first Boeing 707 made its test flight. This airliner went on to become one of the world's best-selling aircraft, carrying millions of people for many different airlines all over the world.

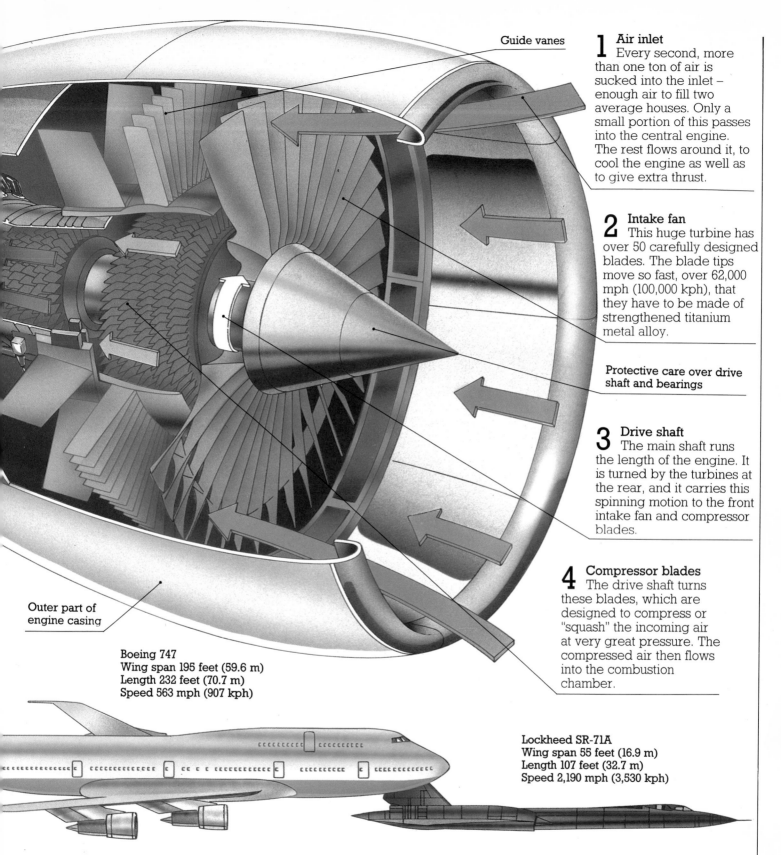

Guide vanes

1 Air inlet
Every second, more than one ton of air is sucked into the inlet – enough air to fill two average houses. Only a small portion of this passes into the central engine. The rest flows around it, to cool the engine as well as to give extra thrust.

2 Intake fan
This huge turbine has over 50 carefully designed blades. The blade tips move so fast, over 62,000 mph (100,000 kph), that they have to be made of strengthened titanium metal alloy.

Protective care over drive shaft and bearings

3 Drive shaft
The main shaft runs the length of the engine. It is turned by the turbines at the rear, and it carries this spinning motion to the front intake fan and compressor blades.

4 Compressor blades
The drive shaft turns these blades, which are designed to compress or "squash" the incoming air at very great pressure. The compressed air then flows into the combustion chamber.

Outer part of engine casing

Boeing 747
Wing span 195 feet (59.6 m)
Length 232 feet (70.7 m)
Speed 563 mph (907 kph)

Lockheed SR-71A
Wing span 55 feet (16.9 m)
Length 107 feet (32.7 m)
Speed 2,190 mph (3,530 kph)

The "Jumbo Jet"
Still the biggest jet airliner, the 747 "Jumbo jet" can transport more than 500 passengers. It came into service during the 1970s. Although it is not particularly fast, it can carry so many people that the price of each air ticket is less than in a smaller plane. The 747 and other wide-bodied giants, such as the Lockheed Tristar, have brought the cost of air travel within reach of many more people.

Lockheed SR-71A "Blackbird"
Modern jet fighters and experimental jet planes fly at incredible speeds. In 1976, the Lockheed SR-71A reached the Mach 3.3, or 3.3 times the speed of sound – 2,190 mph (over 3,500 kph). Its wing span is only slightly more than the E28/39, but it is almost three times longer, and over five times faster. In 1967 the North American X-15 rocket plane reached the speed of 4,534 mph (7,297 kph).

THE PRODUCTION LINE

Wilbur and Orville Wright made the first aircraft themselves with spare pieces of wood and parts from bicycles. Building a modern jetliner, like the Airbus A320 or A340, involves hundreds of specialty manufacturers and thousands of assembly workers. It is an immensely expensive undertaking. Each Airbus is worth over $15 million and the costs of designing and constructing Airbuses are shared between several European nations.

In each country, the separate parts are produced by dozens of subcontractors. The parts are taken to the main contractor where they are built up into larger assemblies, such as a wing or an engine. Airbus assemblies are then flown to Toulouse, in southwest France, where they are fitted together to make the finished plane.

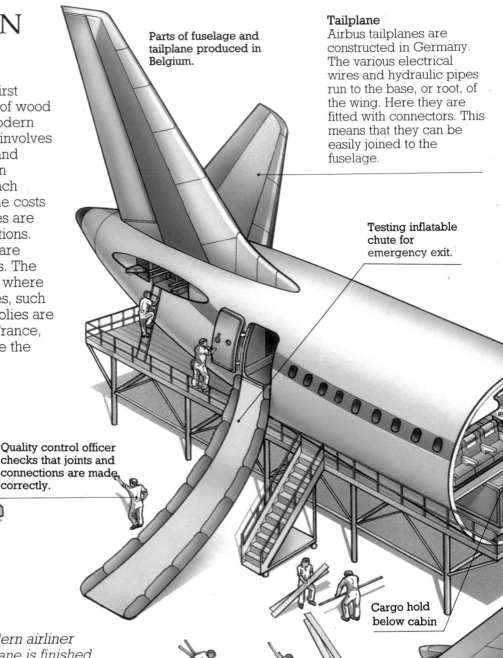

Parts of fuselage and tailplane produced in Belgium.

Tailplane
Airbus tailplanes are constructed in Germany. The various electrical wires and hydraulic pipes run to the base, or root, of the wing. Here they are fitted with connectors. This means that they can be easily joined to the fuselage.

Testing inflatable chute for emergency exit.

Quality control officer checks that joints and connections are made correctly.

Cargo hold below cabin

Building the airbus
The final stages in constructing a modern airliner might look something like this. The plane is finished in a giant hangar, and it is only one of several on the production line, each at a different stage of completion. Boeing's main assembly building near Seattle, in the United States, encloses 200 million cubic feet (5.6 million cu m) – more space than any other building in the world.

Wings
Airbus wings are put together near Bristol, England. The wings, in particular, require much expertise in welding and joining the different kinds of metals used for the spars, ribs, and covering "skin." Cables and pipes are installed for the control surfaces and fuel tanks.

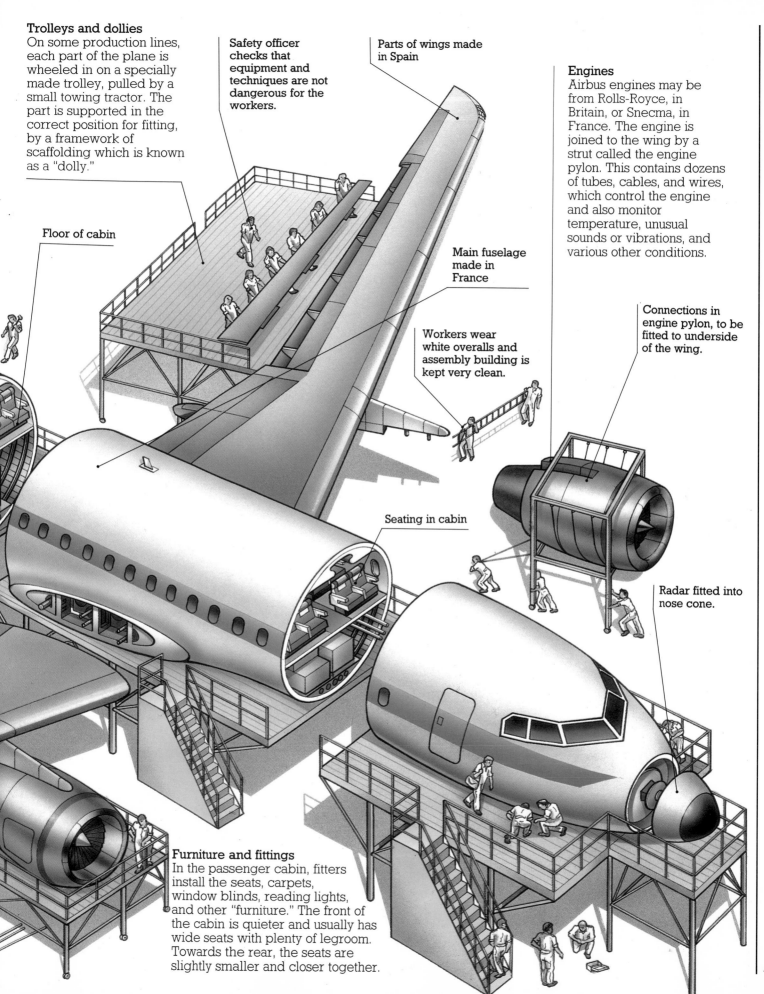

Trolleys and dollies
On some production lines, each part of the plane is wheeled in on a specially made trolley, pulled by a small towing tractor. The part is supported in the correct position for fitting, by a framework of scaffolding which is known as a "dolly."

Safety officer checks that equipment and techniques are not dangerous for the workers.

Parts of wings made in Spain

Engines
Airbus engines may be from Rolls-Royce, in Britain, or Snecma, in France. The engine is joined to the wing by a strut called the engine pylon. This contains dozens of tubes, cables, and wires, which control the engine and also monitor temperature, unusual sounds or vibrations, and various other conditions.

Floor of cabin

Main fuselage made in France

Workers wear white overalls and assembly building is kept very clean.

Connections in engine pylon, to be fitted to underside of the wing.

Seating in cabin

Radar fitted into nose cone.

Furniture and fittings
In the passenger cabin, fitters install the seats, carpets, window blinds, reading lights, and other "furniture." The front of the cabin is quieter and usually has wide seats with plenty of legroom. Towards the rear, the seats are slightly smaller and closer together.

BUS IN THE SKY

The jet airliner purrs smoothly through the sky, carrying 200 passengers in safety and comfort at nearly the speed of sound, 6 miles (10 km) above the Earth. Hundreds of jetliners like this fly around the globe. They transport people, mail, medicines, and other cargoes, when speed is vital.

The first regular airline service began in 1914 in Florida, United States. The single passenger sat next to the pilot in a small two-seater Benoist flying boat, wearing goggles, a helmet, and a flying suit! Today,

the world's major airlines fly a total of 4,650 billion passenger-miles each year.

The airline business employs millions of people, from pilots and cabin crew, to the air traffic controllers who organize takeoffs, flight paths, and landings at the airports, to the ground crew who service and fuel and repair the planes, to the catering staff, to the launderers and cleaners. . . . Thousands of people also work in the design, construction, and testing of new planes.

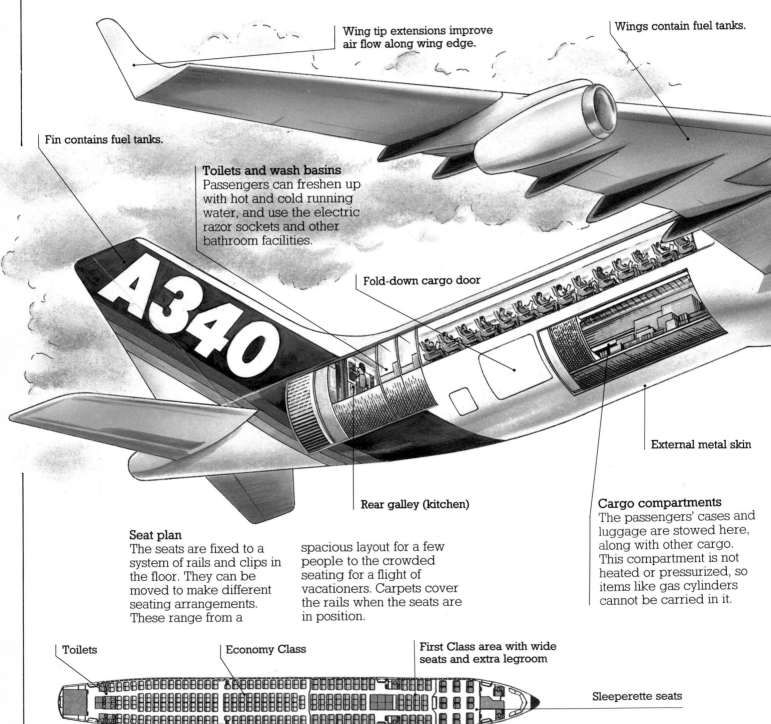

Wing tip extensions improve air flow along wing edge.

Wings contain fuel tanks.

Fin contains fuel tanks.

Toilets and wash basins
Passengers can freshen up with hot and cold running water, and use the electric razor sockets and other bathroom facilities.

Fold-down cargo door

External metal skin

Rear galley (kitchen)

Cargo compartments
The passengers' cases and luggage are stowed here, along with other cargo. This compartment is not heated or pressurized, so items like gas cylinders cannot be carried in it.

Seat plan
The seats are fixed to a system of rails and clips in the floor. They can be moved to make different seating arrangements. These range from a spacious layout for a few people to the crowded seating for a flight of vacationers. Carpets cover the rails when the seats are in position.

Toilets

Economy Class

First Class area with wide seats and extra legroom

Sleeperette seats

Inside the Airbus A340

Today's passenger-carrying flying machine is a masterpiece of design and construction – with safety built in. The passenger cabin is sealed and contains pressurized air. This is necessary because at cruising heights of 32,808 feet (10,000 m) the air outside is very cold and thin. Heaters, air-freshening machines, and humidifiers keep the conditions inside comfortable.

Seats tip back for rest and sleep.

Forward galley

Radar in nose

Foldaway table for each passenger

Cockpit

Multiglazed windows of toughened glass and clear plastic

Nose wheel folded into landing gear compartment.

Emergency exit door

Flight recorder or "black box" (in fact, usually a red cylinder)

Fuselage
The tube-shaped fuselage is built from light metal alloys. The lengthways girders (stringers) and circular hoops make the fuselage extremely strong and rigid.

Forward galley
The galley is the plane's "kitchen." Little cooking is done on most flights, however. The meals are usually prepared by caterers near the airport, loaded in stacks on large containers just before takeoff, and heated prior to being served.

Turbofan jet engines are quiet, smooth-running, and economical on fuel.

Cabin crew
The airline cabin staff look after the passengers. They serve meals and drinks, clear away afterward, provide newspapers and books and blankets, and answer questions about the plane and its flight plan. They are also trained in first aid and emergency action.

Hotel in the sky
One version of the Airbus has up to 22 special reclining seats called sleeperettes. These let the passengers rest and doze in more comfort than in the standard types of seats. On very long flights, there are reserve crew members to take over from the main crew. Off-duty members have a special rest area with bunks and entertainment displays (above).

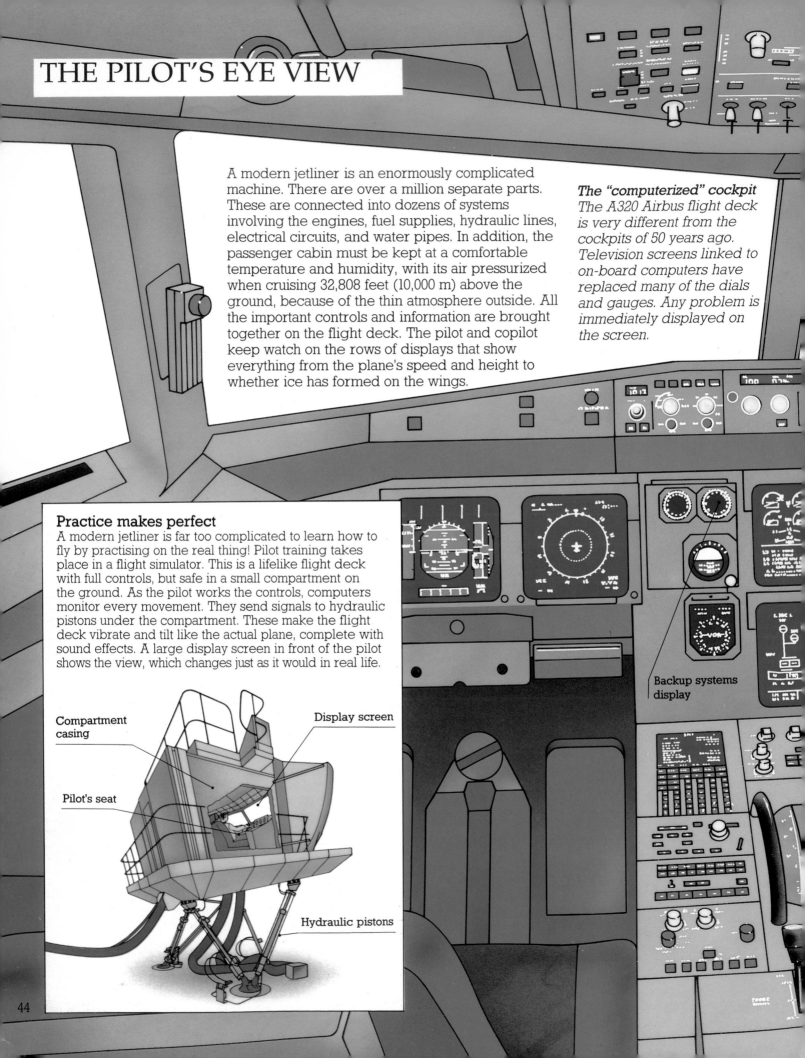

THE PILOT'S EYE VIEW

A modern jetliner is an enormously complicated machine. There are over a million separate parts. These are connected into dozens of systems involving the engines, fuel supplies, hydraulic lines, electrical circuits, and water pipes. In addition, the passenger cabin must be kept at a comfortable temperature and humidity, with its air pressurized when cruising 32,808 feet (10,000 m) above the ground, because of the thin atmosphere outside. All the important controls and information are brought together on the flight deck. The pilot and copilot keep watch on the rows of displays that show everything from the plane's speed and height to whether ice has formed on the wings.

The "computerized" cockpit
The A320 Airbus flight deck is very different from the cockpits of 50 years ago. Television screens linked to on-board computers have replaced many of the dials and gauges. Any problem is immediately displayed on the screen.

Practice makes perfect

A modern jetliner is far too complicated to learn how to fly by practising on the real thing! Pilot training takes place in a flight simulator. This is a lifelike flight deck with full controls, but safe in a small compartment on the ground. As the pilot works the controls, computers monitor every movement. They send signals to hydraulic pistons under the compartment. These make the flight deck vibrate and tilt like the actual plane, complete with sound effects. A large display screen in front of the pilot shows the view, which changes just as it would in real life.

Compartment casing

Display screen

Pilot's seat

Hydraulic pistons

Backup systems display

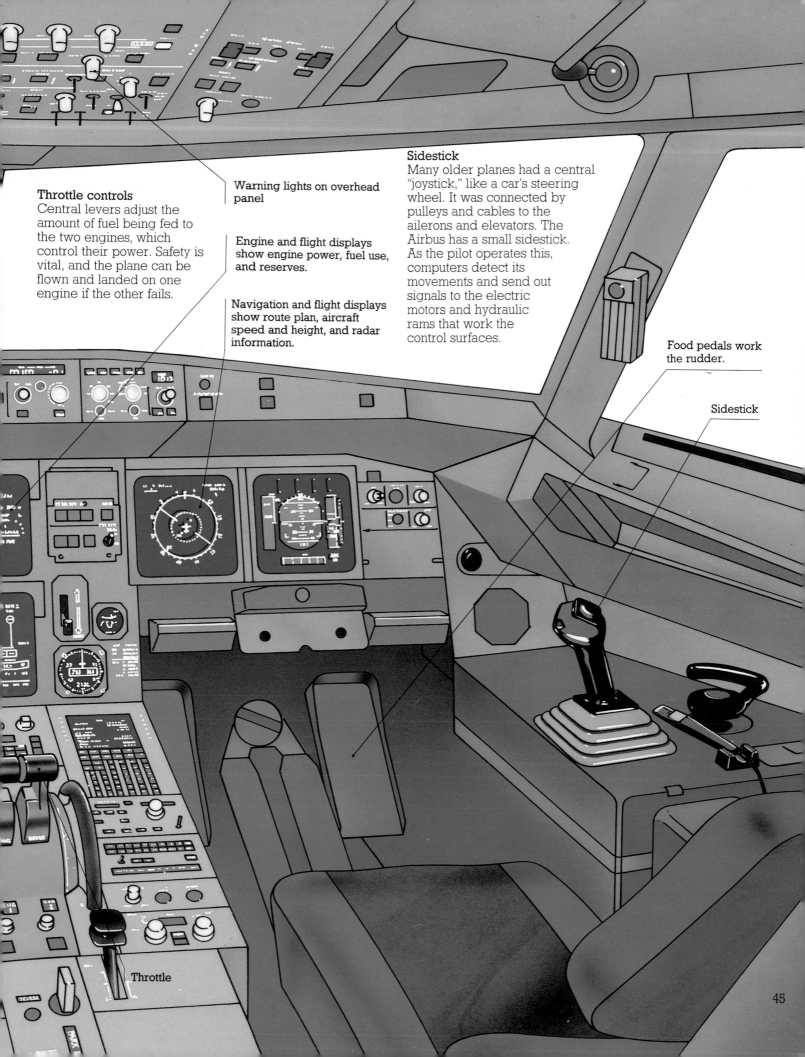

Throttle controls
Central levers adjust the amount of fuel being fed to the two engines, which control their power. Safety is vital, and the plane can be flown and landed on one engine if the other fails.

Warning lights on overhead panel

Engine and flight displays show engine power, fuel use, and reserves.

Navigation and flight displays show route plan, aircraft speed and height, and radar information.

Sidestick
Many older planes had a central "joystick," like a car's steering wheel. It was connected by pulleys and cables to the ailerons and elevators. The Airbus has a small sidestick. As the pilot operates this, computers detect its movements and send out signals to the electric motors and hydraulic rams that work the control surfaces.

Food pedals work the rudder.

Sidestick

Throttle

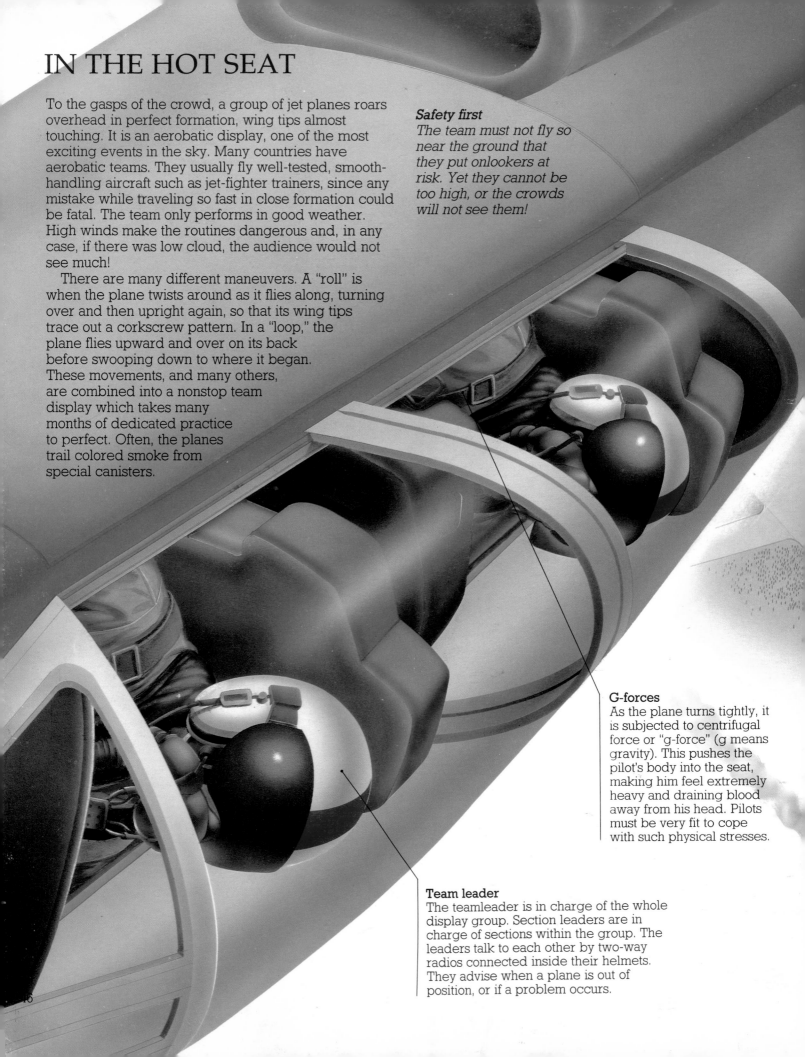

IN THE HOT SEAT

To the gasps of the crowd, a group of jet planes roars overhead in perfect formation, wing tips almost touching. It is an aerobatic display, one of the most exciting events in the sky. Many countries have aerobatic teams. They usually fly well-tested, smooth-handling aircraft such as jet-fighter trainers, since any mistake while traveling so fast in close formation could be fatal. The team only performs in good weather. High winds make the routines dangerous and, in any case, if there was low cloud, the audience would not see much!

There are many different maneuvers. A "roll" is when the plane twists around as it flies along, turning over and then upright again, so that its wing tips trace out a corkscrew pattern. In a "loop," the plane flies upward and over on its back before swooping down to where it began. These movements, and many others, are combined into a nonstop team display which takes many months of dedicated practice to perfect. Often, the planes trail colored smoke from special canisters.

Safety first
The team must not fly so near the ground that they put onlookers at risk. Yet they cannot be too high, or the crowds will not see them!

G-forces
As the plane turns tightly, it is subjected to centrifugal force or "g-force" (g means gravity). This pushes the pilot's body into the seat, making him feel extremely heavy and draining blood away from his head. Pilots must be very fit to cope with such physical stresses.

Team leader
The teamleader is in charge of the whole display group. Section leaders are in charge of sections within the group. The leaders talk to each other by two-way radios connected inside their helmets. They advise when a plane is out of position, or if a problem occurs.

Flight of the falcon

The peregrine falcon is the supreme aerobat. Its eyes can pick out a pigeon over 3 miles (5 km) away, and it twists and turns in midair to catch its prey. This hunter circles on high until it spots a victim. Then it folds back its wings and dives at speeds of over 200 mph (325 kph), plunging its talons into the prey as it plummets past, and returns to pick up the body from the ground. The male peregrine also courts his partner with astonishing aerobatics.

Peregrines catch grouse, pigeons, gulls, and even geese.

The Red Arrows

Britain's Royal Air Force aerobatics team is called the Red Arrows. They fly Hawk jet trainers. A typical performance involves nine planes plus reserves, and lasts for about 20 minutes. They carry out their displays at speeds of up to 350 mph (550 kph).

Slipstreams

As planes fly close together, the ones behind are rocked and swayed by the jet gases and the air streaming past the planes in front. This swirling air behind the leading planes is called the "slipstream."

The Nine Arrow Formation

47

VERTICAL TAKEOFF – AND LANDING!

When fighter planes are locked in deadly battle, speed is not everything. Agility is also vital. The British Aerospace Harrier is not the fastest jet, with a top speed of about 735 mph (1,180 kph). But it is amazingly agile. It can turn extremely quickly, and has the surprising ability to slow down from a speed of almost 600 mph (1,000 kph) to zero in 12 seconds. The Harrier can hover in midair, like a helicopter.

The Harrier is one of a small family of VTOL aircraft, meaning Vertical TakeOff and Landing. It can take off and fly straight upward, and land by coming straight down. It can go sideways and even backward. For this reason it has been nicknamed the "Jump Jet." This is very useful at sea, when landing on the deck of an aircraft carrier. It is an advantage, too, in mountains or jungles. The Harrier needs no runway, simply a small clearing as a base.

Ready for action
A Sea Harrier blasts straight upward from the deck of an aircraft carrier, for a patrol far out at sea. Although Harriers are slower than some combat jets, their amazing agility gives them the edge in battle. In practice against F-15 Eagles, which are much faster, Harriers have won three out of four dogfights.

Fin and rudder
The control surfaces work only when the Harrier is flying forward at speed. When hovering or flying very slowly, the pilot maneuvers the plane by adjusting the angles of the jet nozzles and the power of the engine.

Air intake
The single Rolls-Royce Pegasus jet engine has two air intakes, one on either side of the fuselage just behind the cockpit.

Fuselage and wings
The Harrier is constructed from special combinations of metals or alloys. These are light yet strong. The fuselage is 48 feet (14.5 m) long, and the wingspan 25 feet (7.7 m).

Extra fuel tanks

Fuselage

Wing tip wheels
Because of the swiveling nozzles, there is only one central set of wheels under the fuselage. An ordinary plane has one set on either side. So under each wing tip, the Harrier has a small wheel on a long, shock-absorbing leg. These wheels steady the plane as it takes off and lands, and they fold back when the plane is in level flight.

Nozzles direct jet gases downward.

Main wheels

Single nose wheel

Lift-off

The Harrier's four jet nozzles are on the sides of the fuselage, under the wings. Their angled plates control the direction of the jet exhaust gases. During vertical takeoff (1), the gases flow straight down and push the plane upward. As the Harrier gains height, the nozzles swivel to force the gases down and back, pushing the plane forward (2). At high speed they face backward (3), and the airflow over the wings gives the lift that keeps the plane up (page 34).

3. Fast forward flight

2. Slow forward flight

1. Vertical take-off

STO and VL

The Harrier can lift off vertically, but not when it is fully loaded. In addition, a vertical takeoff uses lots of fuel, and it is a tricky task in high winds on the rocking deck of an aircraft carrier.

More often, the plane is flown with a Short TakeOff run and a Vertical Landing – known as STOVL. For extra help, some aircraft carriers have "ski jump" ramps fitted to their decks. The Harrier speeds forward along the deck and then up the ramp and into the air, like a human ski jumper. STOVL allows the plane to carry a heavier load and quickly gives it good forward speed, so that it is easier to control.

Radar in nose cone

Wing tip wheel

Weapons

Harriers carry various underwing weapons, or extra fuel tanks, depending on their task. A common weapon is the Sidewinder air-to-air missile. This homes in on the hot jet gases of an enemy plane.

The jump insect

A grasshopper takes off and flies in a similar way to a Harrier. It leaps up with its tremendously strong back legs, to gain height and forward speed. Then it spreads its wings, flutters along on these, and glides in to land. You may see the wings of a grasshopper open in a flash of color just after its leap.

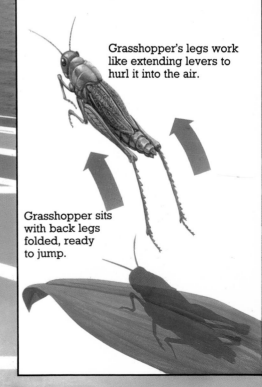

Grasshopper's legs work like extending levers to hurl it into the air.

Grasshopper sits with back legs folded, ready to jump.

WINGS OF TODAY

Aircraft can be used for many and varied jobs. But the same plane would not be suited to every task. Just as we have buses, trucks, family sedans, and sports cars on the road, so there is a variety of planes in the air. Each design is a complex mixture of many factors: good aerodynamics, safety, carrying ability, speed, fuel economy, range (the distance it can fly without refueling), comfort, and, of course, cost. Concorde's cruising speed of 1,355 mph (2,180 kph) helps people get around the world fast, but at a price. It is a relatively noisy plane and needs a long runway, so it has to use big airports away from cities. The Dash 7's short takeoff run and quiet engines allow it to do short hops from one city center to another, which is convenient for business travelers. Medium-sized, medium-range jets like the Boeing 737 are the "workhorses" of the air routes. They fly regular trips to many different airports.

Designed for their jobs

All these aircraft are built on the same basic plan, with a fuselage, wings, fin, and engines. However, each plane is a certain size and shape to suit a specific task. A Boeing 747 carries 500 passengers across the Atlantic in seven hours. The 130-seater Concorde takes only three hours – but each ticket costs a lot more!

Superfast

Concorde began carrying passengers regularly in 1976. It is powered by four Rolls-Royce Olympus jet engines slung under the "delta" wing. The delta shape is taken from the Greek letter [Δ]. Concorde cruises at more than 60,000 feet above the Earth.

Concorde

Superslow

The Optica is specially designed to fly very slowly, at speeds of only 30 mph (50 kph). It is an observation and survey "spotter" plane. It can do similar jobs to a helicopter, but it costs much less.

Optica

Superquiet

The Dash 7 is a 50-seater passenger plane that can take off from the very short runways of city "STOLports" (Short TakeOff and Landing Ports). It is extremely quiet and climbs steeply into the air. This means that it causes little noise disturbance to people living nearby.

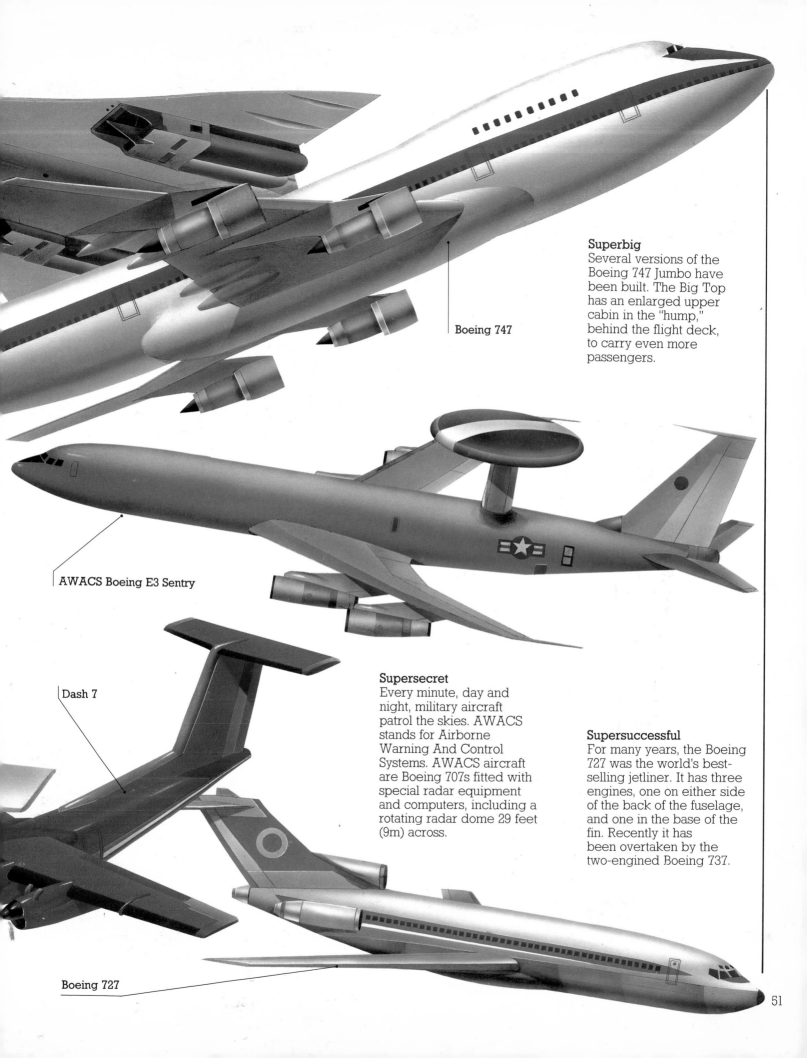

Boeing 747

Superbig
Several versions of the Boeing 747 Jumbo have been built. The Big Top has an enlarged upper cabin in the "hump," behind the flight deck, to carry even more passengers.

AWACS Boeing E3 Sentry

Dash 7

Supersecret
Every minute, day and night, military aircraft patrol the skies. AWACS stands for Airborne Warning And Control Systems. AWACS aircraft are Boeing 707s fitted with special radar equipment and computers, including a rotating radar dome 29 feet (9m) across.

Supersuccessful
For many years, the Boeing 727 was the world's best-selling jetliner. It has three engines, one on either side of the back of the fuselage, and one in the base of the fin. Recently it has been overtaken by the two-engined Boeing 737.

Boeing 727

AIR AND SEA

Aircraft and helicopters are well-suited to guarding our coastlines and saving people in danger at sea, from a child stranded on a airfloat, to the crew of a sinking ship. Aircraft fly regular patrols, known as "maritime reconnaissance," up and down the coast. The crews watch for emergencies or suspicious boats that may be being used for smuggling. Helicopters cannot fly as far or fast as planes, but they can hover above the waves and lift people to safety. In most countries, such work is carried out by the Coast Guard service. The United States Coast Guard has over 40,000 staff and is equipped with its own aircraft and helicopters.

No escape
This smugglers' boat was spotted by a United States Coast Guard plane on routine patrol. The helicopter was called in, and after a high-speed chase, the criminals have realized that there is no escape. The helicopter crewman shouts through a megaphone, advising them to surrender.

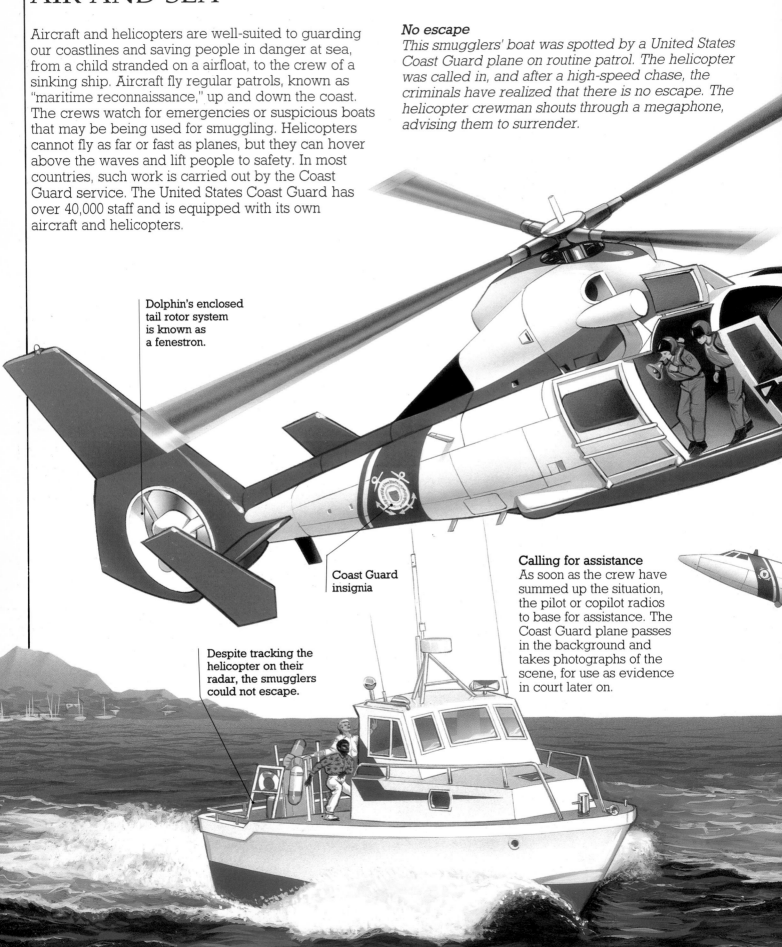

Dolphin's enclosed tail rotor system is known as a fenestron.

Coast Guard insignia

Despite tracking the helicopter on their radar, the smugglers could not escape.

Calling for assistance
As soon as the crew have summed up the situation, the pilot or copilot radios to base for assistance. The Coast Guard plane passes in the background and takes photographs of the scene, for use as evidence in court later on.

Seaplanes

An airport runway, made of tough tarmac, long and firm and flat, costs a large amount of money and takes up a great deal of space. The sea is a vast, open expanse which seaplanes can use as a "runway." The seaplane's boat-shaped fuselage and stabilizing wing floats allow it to skim over the surface and come to rest near a harbor or jetty. Seaplanes are most useful in regions where there are many small islands, with little room to build proper runways. One drawback is that they cannot operate in rough weather. Big waves make takeoff and landing too dangerous for the aircraft.

The seaplane has wheels that fold out from beneath the engines. With its wheels down, it can float through the water and then roll up a ramp on to the shore.

Wing floats keep the plane steady in the water.

"SAR"

The Aerospatiale HH-65A Dolphin helicopter is a specialized SAR aircraft, meaning "Search and Rescue." It is painted in bright colors, so that it can be seen easily by people stranded at sea.

Dassault-Breguet HU-25A Guardian, the Coast Guard patrol plane on "maritime reconnaissance," which spotted the smugglers.

Steering clear

Only boats from the Coast Guard, police, or armed forces should approach the criminals. Radio messages on the general "hailing frequency" warn ordinary boats to stay away, in case there is any shooting.

Launch radar detects approach of helicopter.

THE "ROTARY WING"

The wings of a normal aircraft are fixed to its fuselage. This is known as the "fixed-wing" design, and the wings only create a lifting force when the whole plane moves through the air (page 34). A helicopter's wings are, in effect, the long rotor blades that twirl around on top. As the blades rotate, they push air down past them, pulling the craft upward. The lift is generated even if the helicopter's body is stationary, because the rotors are still swirling around and pushing air past them. This is why helicopters can hover in midair. It is also why they are often called "rotary-winged" aircraft. The word "helicopter" comes from two Greek words, *helix* meaning "spiral," and *pteron* meaning "wing." Helicopter pilots must pass their own tests in order to obtain a rotary-wing flying license, since the helicopter's controls and the way it is flown are quite different from a fixed-wing aircraft.

Lynx on patrol
The Westland Super Lynx is a fast, modern, and adaptable helicopter. In particular, it is intended to fly from aircraft carriers and other navy ships, on the lookout for enemy boats, aircraft, and submarines.

Main rotors
Unlike the all-metal rotor blades of some older helicopters, the Lynx's rotors are made from newly developed "composite" materials. These are combinations of metals and other substances, such as carbon fiber, a material which is light and flexible yet strong.

Rotor design
The rotor blade has been designed with the help of computers. It has an enlarged "paddle" tip, and its shape and flexibility vary along its length, for greater lifting power.

The Super Lynx has a new semi-rigid rotor head that transfers more power to the rotors.

Pilot
On-board computerized controls keep a check on fuel levels and the engine condition.

The first helicopter
The world's first helicopter pilot was Paul Cornu, a French inventor. He designed the machine himself, and made it chiefly from bicycle parts. On November 13, 1907, he sat at the controls and took off on a flight lasting only 20 seconds, hovering just 1 foot (30 cm) above the ground. On later flights he managed to reach the dizzy height of almost 7 feet (2 m)! The first successful, fully steerable, single-rotor helicopter was developed and flown by the Russian-born designer Igor Sikorsky in 1939, in the United States.

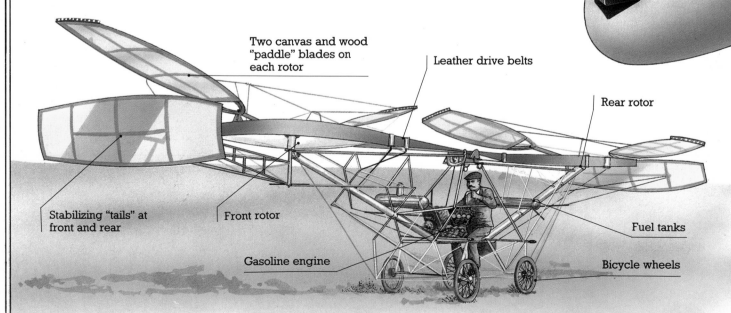

Two canvas and wood "paddle" blades on each rotor

Leather drive belts

Rear rotor

Stabilizing "tails" at front and rear

Front rotor

Fuel tanks

Gasoline engine

Bicycle wheels

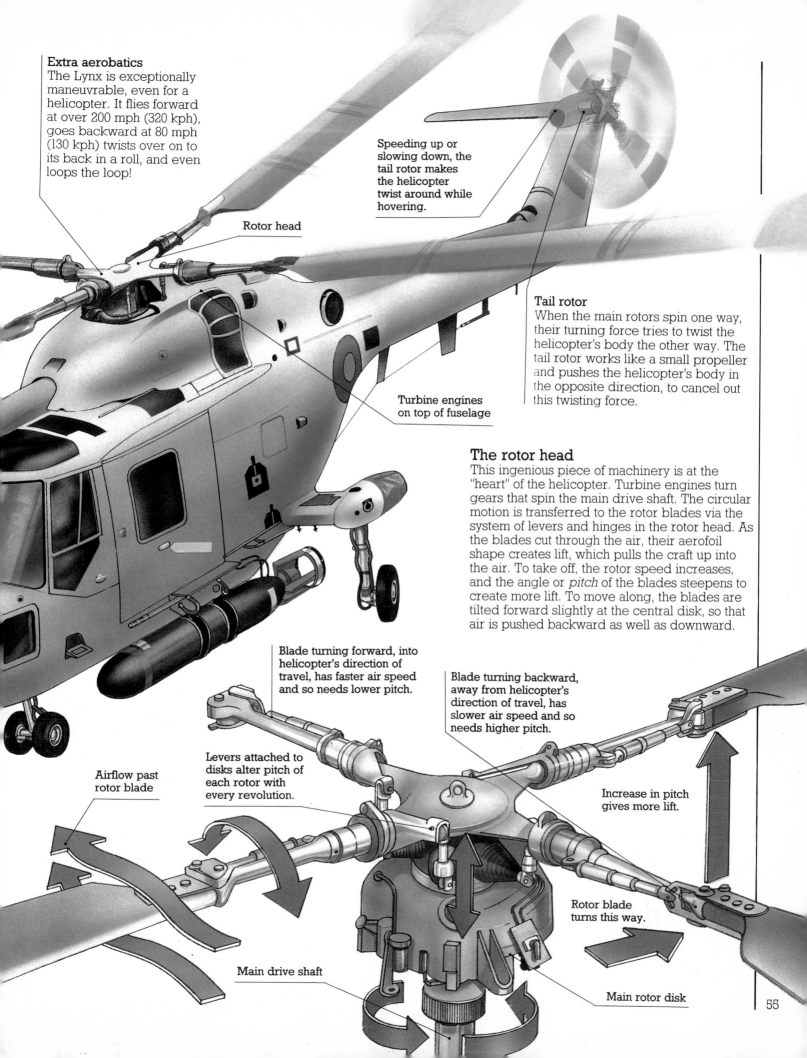

Extra aerobatics
The Lynx is exceptionally maneuvrable, even for a helicopter. It flies forward at over 200 mph (320 kph), goes backward at 80 mph (130 kph) twists over on to its back in a roll, and even loops the loop!

Rotor head

Speeding up or slowing down, the tail rotor makes the helicopter twist around while hovering.

Tail rotor
When the main rotors spin one way, their turning force tries to twist the helicopter's body the other way. The tail rotor works like a small propeller and pushes the helicopter's body in the opposite direction, to cancel out this twisting force.

Turbine engines on top of fuselage

The rotor head
This ingenious piece of machinery is at the "heart" of the helicopter. Turbine engines turn gears that spin the main drive shaft. The circular motion is transferred to the rotor blades via the system of levers and hinges in the rotor head. As the blades cut through the air, their aerofoil shape creates lift, which pulls the craft up into the air. To take off, the rotor speed increases, and the angle or *pitch* of the blades steepens to create more lift. To move along, the blades are tilted forward slightly at the central disk, so that air is pushed backward as well as downward.

Blade turning forward, into helicopter's direction of travel, has faster air speed and so needs lower pitch.

Blade turning backward, away from helicopter's direction of travel, has slower air speed and so needs higher pitch.

Levers attached to disks alter pitch of each rotor with every revolution.

Increase in pitch gives more lift.

Airflow past rotor blade

Rotor blade turns this way.

Main drive shaft

Main rotor disk

WHIRLING THROUGH THE SKIES

As the rotor blades of a helicopter whirl around and around, they cut through the air with a "chop-chop-chop" sound. This has given helicopters the nickname of "choppers." In the same way that there are many designs of aircraft, suited to different tasks (page 50), there are also many sizes and shapes of "choppers." They are used by the police, coast guard, and armed forces, and for passenger services, weather and traffic reports, aerial surveys, and emergency rescue. They ferry people and freight to and from oil rigs and ships, carry out crop-spraying, fire fighting, air displays, and are used as air ambulances. One of the helicopter's main advantages over a plane is that it does not need a runway to land on, or even a flat patch of tarmac. It only requires a fairly smooth and firm piece of ground – the "landing pad" – with no tall trees or buildings too near. There are more than 20,000 helicopters in the United States alone.

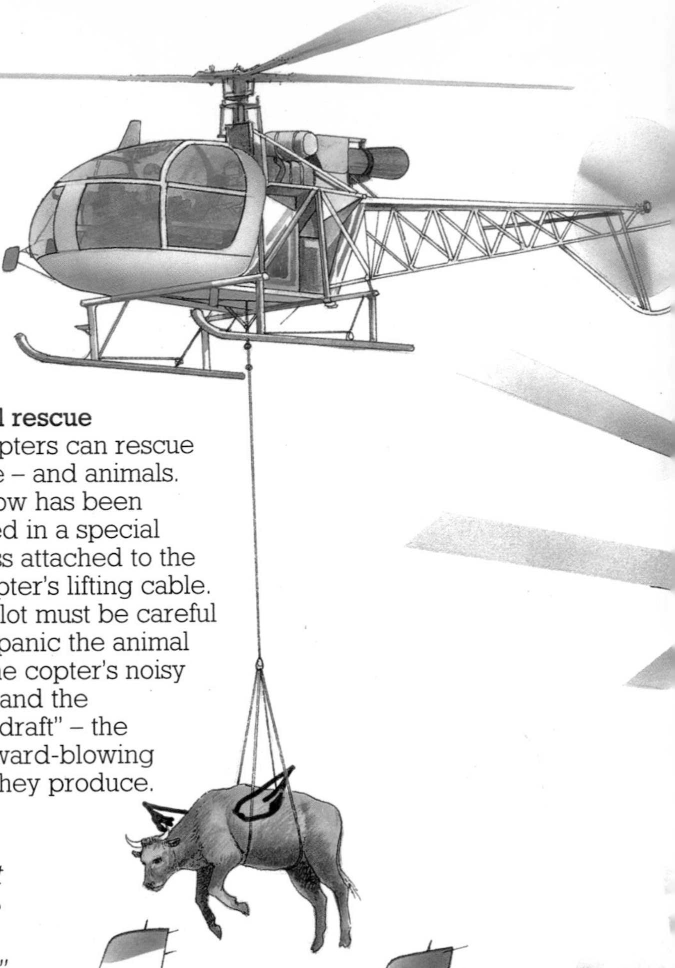

Animal rescue
Helicopters can rescue people – and animals. This cow has been secured in a special harness attached to the helicopter's lifting cable. The pilot must be careful not to panic the animal with the copter's noisy rotors and the "downdraft" – the downward-blowing wind they produce.

"Choppers" at work
The tiny one-person autogyro is used mainly for sport and leisure flying. At the other end of the scale, huge helicopters such as the military Boeing Chinook and the Soviet Mil Mi-26 are "heavy lifters" or "skycranes." The Mi-26 can pick up loads of more than 50 tons.

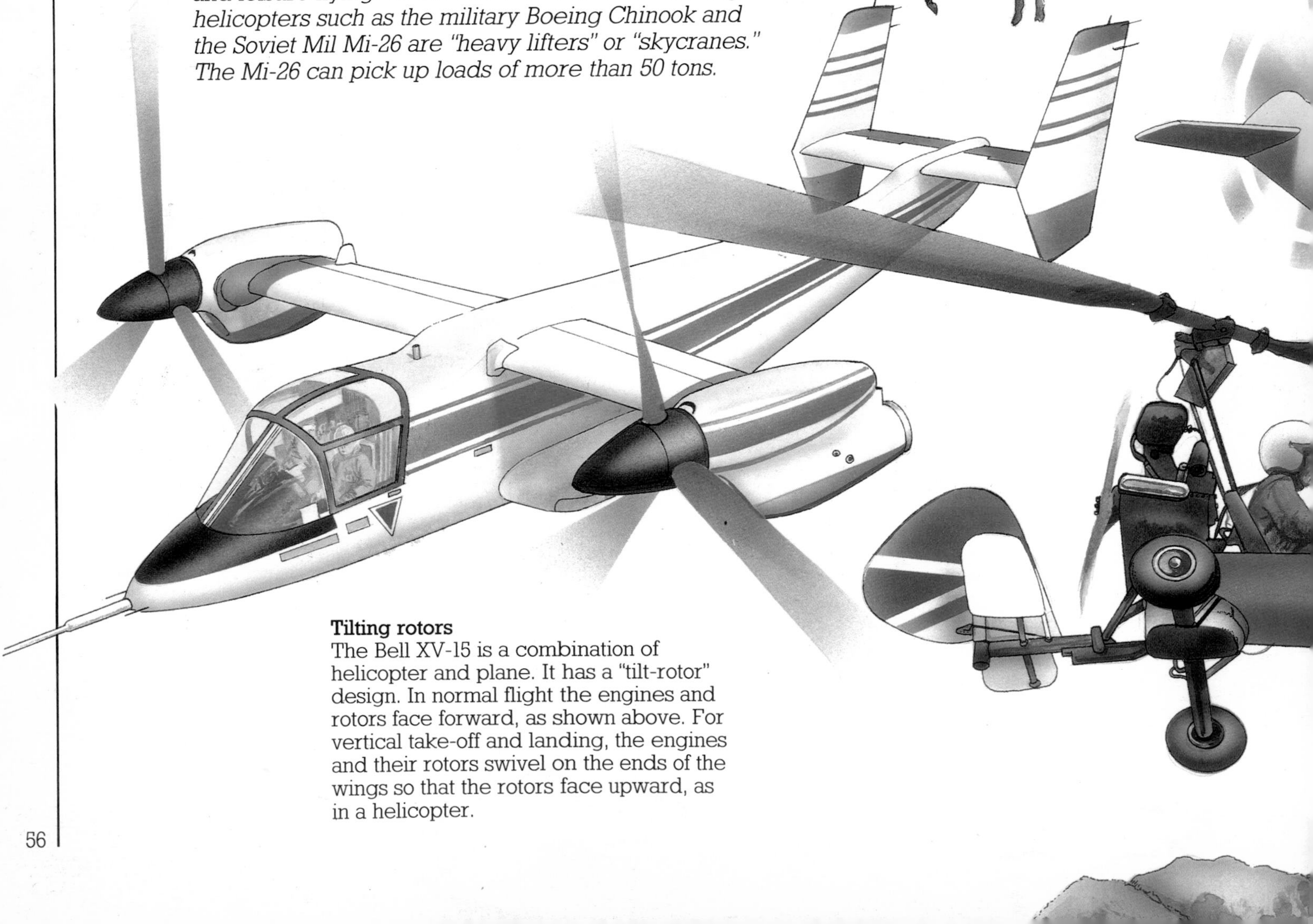

Tilting rotors
The Bell XV-15 is a combination of helicopter and plane. It has a "tilt-rotor" design. In normal flight the engines and rotors face forward, as shown above. For vertical take-off and landing, the engines and their rotors swivel on the ends of the wings so that the rotors face upward, as in a helicopter.

Twin-rotor 234
The Boeing 234 is the passenger-carrying version of the military Chinook. It can transport nearly 50 people in comfort and can "hop" from one city-center landing pad to another. This saves the time that would be spent traveling to large out-of-city airports. The two rotors are linked by gears so that they twirl in unison and do not clash.

Attack "helicopter gunship"
Attack helicopters such as the American Apache (shown here), Soviet Hind, and European Lynx can be fitted with missiles, guns, and bombs. The "gunship" hovers behind rocks or trees, before rising and swooping over the enemy.

Swirling rotor
The autogyro's rotor is not powered. As the craft picks up speed on the runway, pushed by its propeller, the air rushing past makes the rotor spin. Autogyros can cruise at about 100 mph (160 kph).

Air-sea rescue
Sea Kings are used around the world by air forces and coast guards, to help people stranded at sea and also in the mountains. The lifting cable is wound up by a winch and pulley, on the side of the fuselage above the large door. The Sea King was first designed as an antisubmarine helicopter. If it has to "ditch" in the water, its boat-shaped, watertight fuselage can float for a time.

57

INTO SPACE

Flying in space is different from flying near to the surface of the Earth, for several reasons. There is no air in space. So, first, propellers would not work, since they must push air backward to make the craft go forward. Second, control surfaces, such as the rudder, would not be effective, because there is no air for them to push against and make the craft change direction. Third, the various types of combustion and jet engines would not work. They need oxygen, in air, to burn their fuel. Fourth, the Earth's gravity is so weak in space that a craft no longer needs lots of lift (see page 34).

A rocket engine usually carries liquid fuel in huge tanks. In addition it carries its own oxygen in extremely cold liquid form or some other chemical to serve as an oxidizer. The fuel and oxidizer are called propellants. As they burn, hot exhaust gases rush from the back of the rocket. This pushes the craft forward according to the basic law of physics: "Every action has an equal and opposite reaction."

"We have first stage separation. . . ."
To get away from the pull of the Earth's gravity, a spacecraft must reach the "orbital velocity" speed of 17,500 mph (28,175 kph). This takes incredible amounts of power. In a multistage rocket, such as Ariane, the biggest engines boost the craft away from the launch pad. When their fuel runs out they fall away, making the craft lighter, and the smaller next stage takes over.

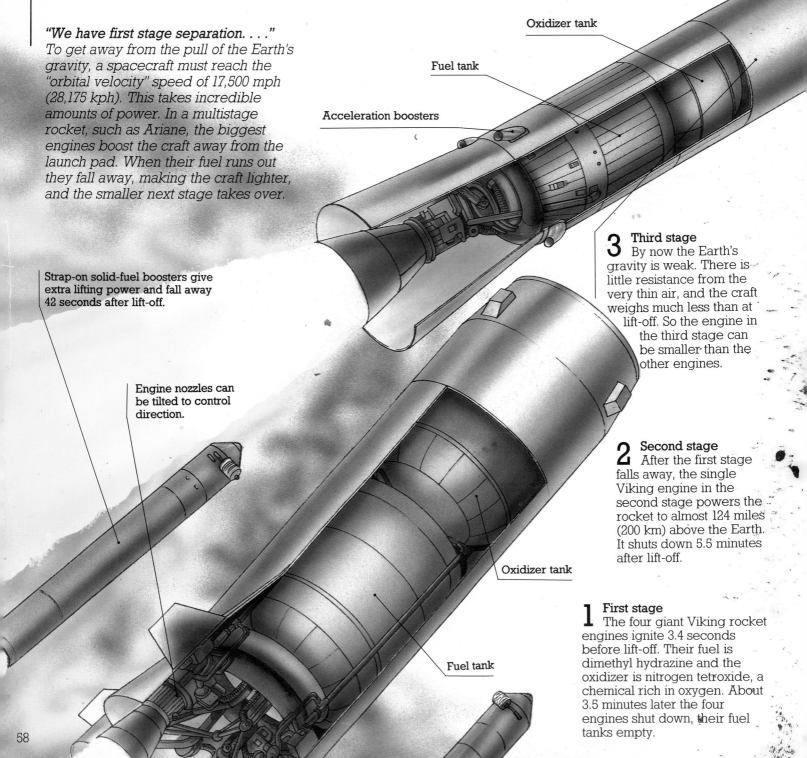

Oxidizer tank

Fuel tank

Acceleration boosters

Strap-on solid-fuel boosters give extra lifting power and fall away 42 seconds after lift-off.

Engine nozzles can be tilted to control direction.

Oxidizer tank

Fuel tank

3 Third stage
By now the Earth's gravity is weak. There is little resistance from the very thin air, and the craft weighs much less than at lift-off. So the engine in the third stage can be smaller than the other engines.

2 Second stage
After the first stage falls away, the single Viking engine in the second stage powers the rocket to almost 124 miles (200 km) above the Earth. It shuts down 5.5 minutes after lift-off.

1 First stage
The four giant Viking rocket engines ignite 3.4 seconds before lift-off. Their fuel is dimethyl hydrazine and the oxidizer is nitrogen tetroxide, a chemical rich in oxygen. About 3.5 minutes later the four engines shut down, their fuel tanks empty.

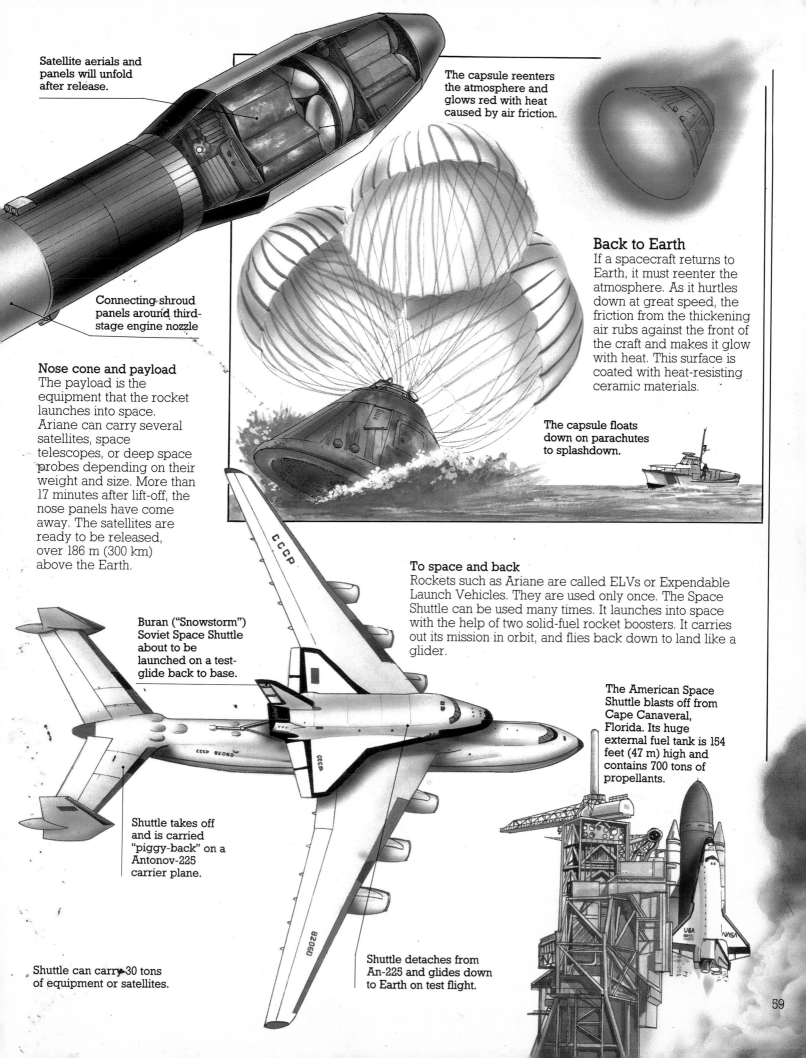

Satellite aerials and panels will unfold after release.

Connecting shroud panels around third-stage engine nozzle

Nose cone and payload
The payload is the equipment that the rocket launches into space. Ariane can carry several satellites, space telescopes, or deep space probes depending on their weight and size. More than 17 minutes after lift-off, the nose panels have come away. The satellites are ready to be released, over 186 m (300 km) above the Earth.

The capsule reenters the atmosphere and glows red with heat caused by air friction.

Back to Earth
If a spacecraft returns to Earth, it must reenter the atmosphere. As it hurtles down at great speed, the friction from the thickening air rubs against the front of the craft and makes it glow with heat. This surface is coated with heat-resisting ceramic materials.

The capsule floats down on parachutes to splashdown.

To space and back
Rockets such as Ariane are called ELVs or Expendable Launch Vehicles. They are used only once. The Space Shuttle can be used many times. It launches into space with the help of two solid-fuel rocket boosters. It carries out its mission in orbit, and flies back down to land like a glider.

Buran ("Snowstorm") Soviet Space Shuttle about to be launched on a test-glide back to base.

The American Space Shuttle blasts off from Cape Canaveral, Florida. Its huge external fuel tank is 154 feet (47 m) high and contains 700 tons of propellants.

Shuttle takes off and is carried "piggy-back" on a Antonov-225 carrier plane.

Shuttle can carry 30 tons of equipment or satellites.

Shuttle detaches from An-225 and glides down to Earth on test flight.

PILOT FOR A DAY

Few people can afford to buy their own plane. But you can become a "pilot" without a real aircraft. One way is to take up an aerial sport such as hang gliding, gliding, or paragliding. There are clubs in most regions, where learners can borrow or hire the craft and have lessons.

Another way is to fly a model aircraft. There are two main kinds. The first is the "scale model," which is based on a real aircraft and copied in every detail. However, for a scale model to fly well, its dimensions may have to be altered slightly. This is because the balance and stability of the small version, and the airflow past its wings and control surfaces, are different from the full-sized craft. The second kind is designed and built purely to fly as well as possible. Such models are capable of astounding aerobatics at speeds of well over 150 mph (240 kph)!

"Pilots" at play

Summer vacations at the coast are an ideal time for sport and leisure flying. The open sea provides plenty of space, while the steady breeze and the updrafts along cliffs give opportunities for gliding and soaring. The flyers can spend all their vacation time at the controls.

Aeromodeling

Just like a real plane, the typical radio-controlled plane has a rudder, elevators, and ailerons. These are moved by stiff wire levers worked by small, light, battery-powered electric motors known as servos. The pilot's controls are on the handheld transmitter. The radio signals are sent from the transmitter to the receiver in the model's fuselage, which controls the servos. Propeller model planes are powered by small internal combustion engines.

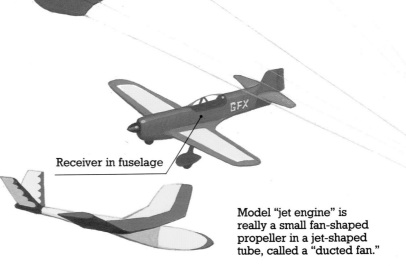

Receiver in fuselage

Model "jet engine" is really a small fan-shaped propeller in a jet-shaped tube, called a "ducted fan."

Transmitter

Antenna

Hang gliders soar in coastal updrafts. (pages 24-25)

Many ultralights are built from kits, or designed and built by their owners (although they must have an official certificate of airworthiness).

Gliders search for thermals. (pages 26-27)

In paragliding, the takeoff is from water skis, and a skilled flyer can land this way, too.

Microlights and ultralights

The microlight is little more than a hang glider (page 24) with a seat and an engine. The ultralight is a very small and light plane, weighing less than 250 pounds (112 kg). Despite their small size and few controls, these machines need skill to fly. Because the craft is so light, the pilot's weight and body position are much more important than in a bigger, heavier plane. Microlights, like hang gliders, can be packed up and stowed in a van or on a trailer, for transport. They are within the price range of many families and groups of keen flyers.

The speed boat picks up paragliders who have had a "heavy landing."

Biplane pulling advertising banner.

US AIRFORCE

Paragliding

Parachutes cannot go upward, unless they are towed behind a speedboat! Paragliding, also called parascending, has become a popular seaside sport in recent years. The person-carrying parachute on its cable works like a kite on its line (pages 20-21). However, the ordinary wind does not provide the lifting force. The forward speed of the boat creates a much stronger "wind," which blows into the parachute and lifts it into the air.

61

AMAZING PLANES

It is less than a century since the Wright brothers first conquered the air with a self-propelled, heavier-than-air, controllable flying machine. Today we have thousands of kinds of aircraft, from ultralights to heavy bombers. Most countries have an air force, and the military need to "stay on top" creates aircraft that fly ever faster and farther. Most cities have an airport, and air travel is part of daily life for many.

However, we are now beginning to recognize the problems that flying machines cause. There is air and noise pollution. Designing and building new planes uses up valuable minerals and other resources, as well as costing vast amounts of money. The Earth's oil, from which we make aviation fuel, will not last forever.

Solving these problems will bring change. Passenger aircraft are becoming quieter, more economical, and safer. There are still challenges to be conquered – especially in the area of human-powered flight.

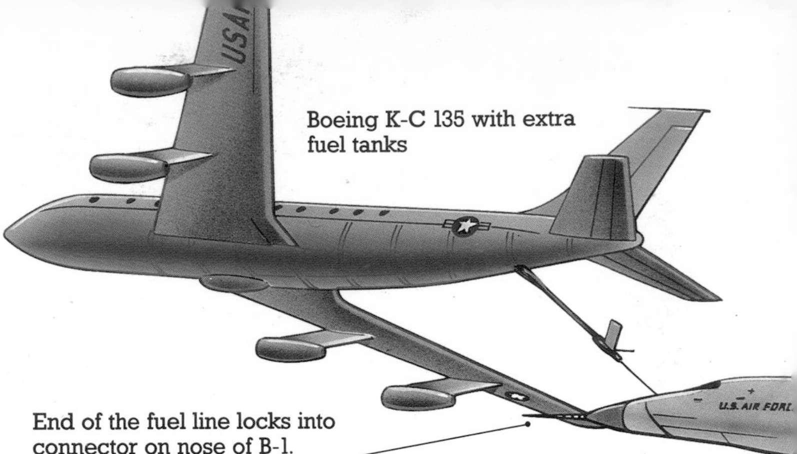

From pedal-power to superstealth
The craft shown here are all record breakers in their own field of flying. At one end of the scale is pedal-driven Daedalus, *named from the inventor of Greek legend, which recreated his escape flight from Crete (page 12). At the other end of the scale, the US Air Force's B-2 "Stealth" bombers are the most sophisticated and expensive flying machines ever. The price tag is $500 million – each!*

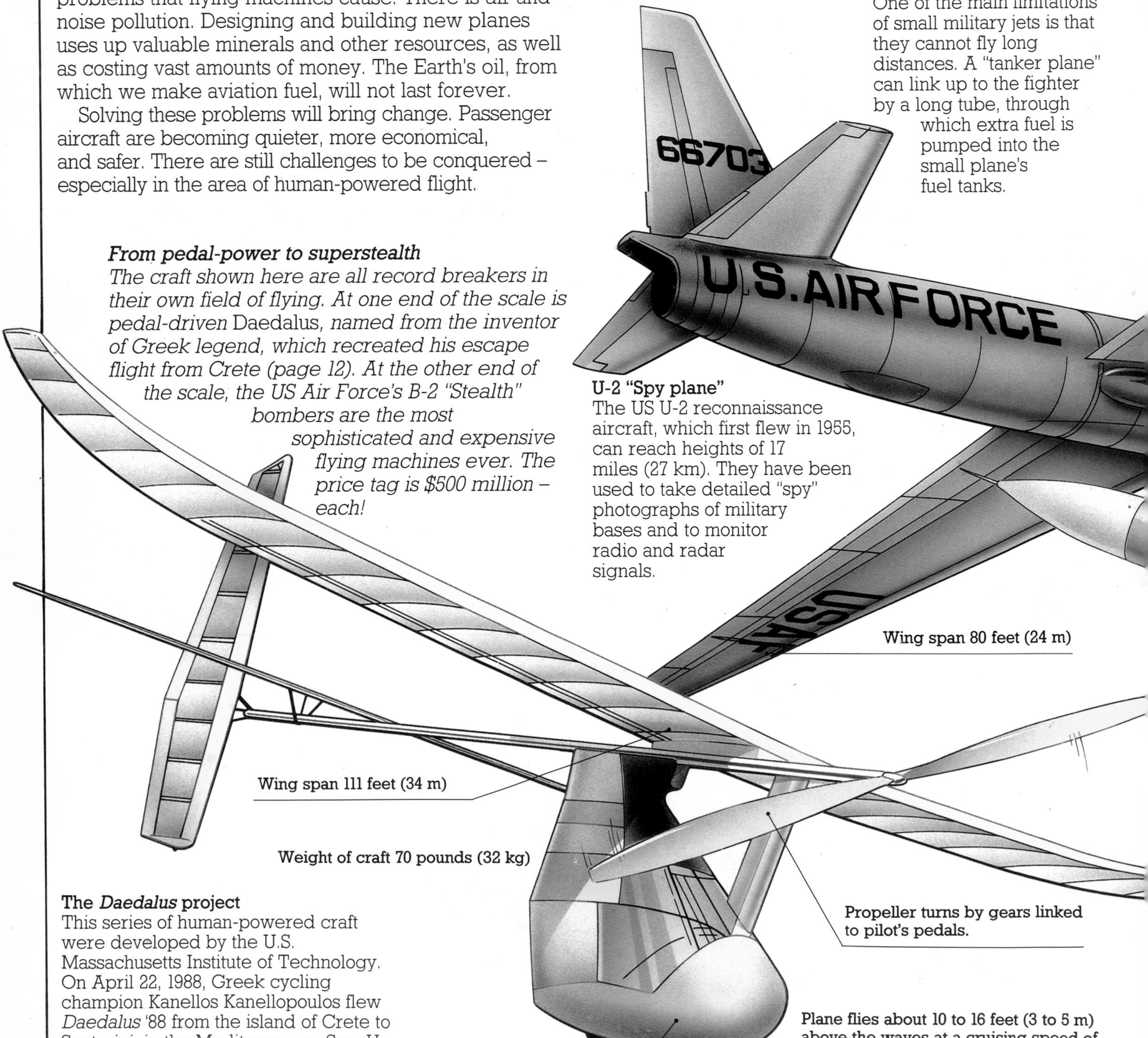

Boeing K-C 135 with extra fuel tanks

End of the fuel line locks into connector on nose of B-1.

Midair refueling
One of the main limitations of small military jets is that they cannot fly long distances. A "tanker plane" can link up to the fighter by a long tube, through which extra fuel is pumped into the small plane's fuel tanks.

66703

U.S.AIR FORCE

U-2 "Spy plane"
The US U-2 reconnaissance aircraft, which first flew in 1955, can reach heights of 17 miles (27 km). They have been used to take detailed "spy" photographs of military bases and to monitor radio and radar signals.

Wing span 80 feet (24 m)

Wing span 111 feet (34 m)

Weight of craft 70 pounds (32 kg)

The *Daedalus* project
This series of human-powered craft were developed by the U.S. Massachusetts Institute of Technology. On April 22, 1988, Greek cycling champion Kanellos Kanellopoulos flew *Daedalus* '88 from the island of Crete to Santorini, in the Mediterranean Sea. He took 3 hours 55 minutes to cover the 74 miles (119 km).

Propeller turns by gears linked to pilot's pedals.

Plane flies about 10 to 16 feet (3 to 5 m) above the waves at a cruising speed of 15.6 mph (24 kph).

Polyester plastic "skin"

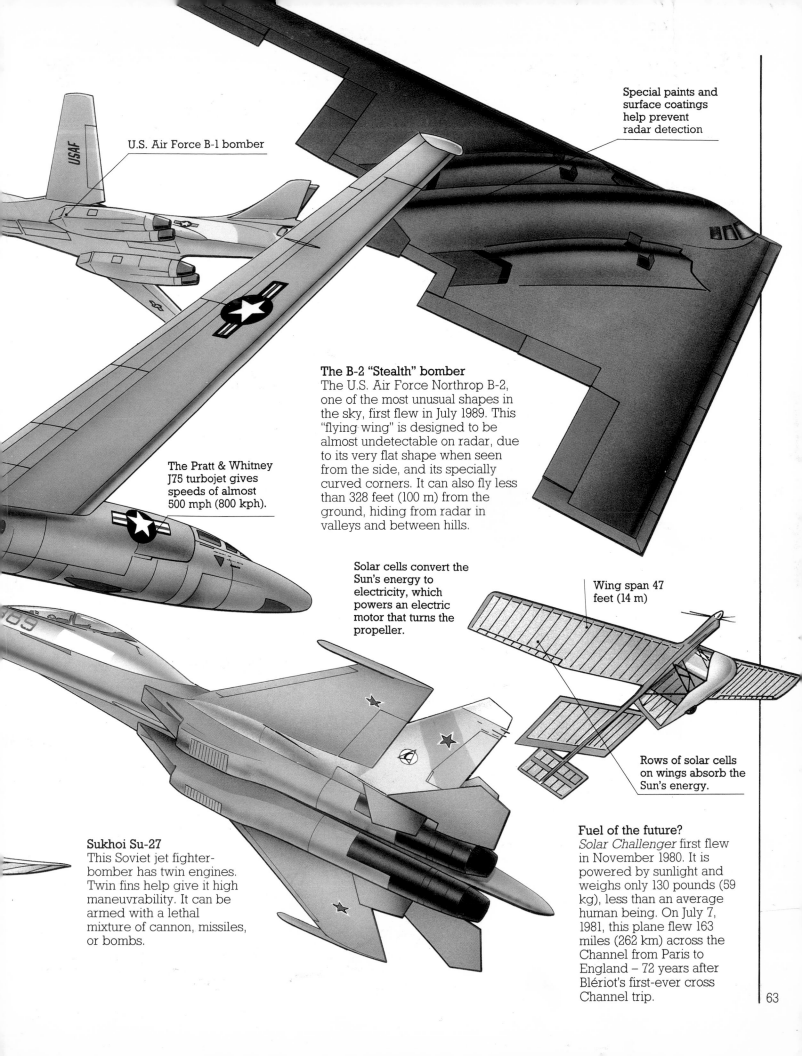

U.S. Air Force B-1 bomber

Special paints and surface coatings help prevent radar detection

The Pratt & Whitney J75 turbojet gives speeds of almost 500 mph (800 kph).

The B-2 "Stealth" bomber
The U.S. Air Force Northrop B-2, one of the most unusual shapes in the sky, first flew in July 1989. This "flying wing" is designed to be almost undetectable on radar, due to its very flat shape when seen from the side, and its specially curved corners. It can also fly less than 328 feet (100 m) from the ground, hiding from radar in valleys and between hills.

Solar cells convert the Sun's energy to electricity, which powers an electric motor that turns the propeller.

Wing span 47 feet (14 m)

Rows of solar cells on wings absorb the Sun's energy.

Sukhoi Su-27
This Soviet jet fighter-bomber has twin engines. Twin fins help give it high maneuvrability. It can be armed with a lethal mixture of cannon, missiles, or bombs.

Fuel of the future?
Solar Challenger first flew in November 1980. It is powered by sunlight and weighs only 130 pounds (59 kg), less than an average human being. On July 7, 1981, this plane flew 163 miles (262 km) across the Channel from Paris to England – 72 years after Blériot's first-ever cross Channel trip.

INDEX

Acknowledgements
Dorling Kindersley would like to thank Don Bentley; Black Hat
Agency; Lynn Bresler; British Aerospace; Canadair; City Airports,
London; Customs and Excise, Dover; David Gefferis; Irvin Great
Britain Ltd, Letchworth; Chris Nall; the RAF Red Arrows; Fred Ray;
Redifusion Simulators Ltd; Suffolk Gliding Club, Ipswich; Virgin
Atlantic Airways; and Westland Helicopters for their help in
producing this book.